The Twin Flame Lover
of China and Denmark

Defang Wan

Copyright © 2016 by Defang Wan
All rights reserved. No part of this publication may be reproduced without permission, stored in a retrieval system or transmitted in any form or by any means, electronic, mechanical, photocopying, recording or otherwise without prior written permission from the copyright owner.

ISBN: 978-0-9979047-0-3

KORA
PRESS

Printed in the United States of America

The Twin Flame Lover
of China and Denmark

Defang Wan

CONTENTS

About the Cover	9
Preface	11
Acknowledgement	13
Twin Flame Reunion Poem	15
Brief Introduction	17

STAGE ONE
Recognition—Love in Heaven
(July 2009-February 2010)

Chapter 1: Recognition of the Soul	21
Chapter 2: English, the Magical Beginning of Everything	33
Chapter 3: Love Stayed, Love Left	39
Chapter 4: Love Torn Asunder, Love Came Back	49
Chapter 5: Moving to Beijing Double Happiness Courtyard Hotel	53

STAGE TWO
Ego Emerging
(February 2010-December 2010)

Chapter 6: Happy New Year! I invited You to My Home Town	61
Chapter 7: We Are Very Confused!	67
Chapter 8: Goodbye Forever???	75
Chapter 9: The Crisis Continues	81

STAGE THREE
Temporary Return
(December 2010-August 2011)

Chapter 10: The Book and the Return	89
Chapter 11: The Six Presents, the Fourth Separation	97
Chapter 12: *The Alchemist* and the Au Pair Dream	101

STAGE FOUR
The Runner and the Chaser
(August 2011-January 2013)

Chapter 13: The Soul-Level Abandonment From Me to You	109
Chapter 14: You Run Away, I Run Around	113
Chapter 15: Return to Double Happiness Courtyard Hotel	119
Chapter 16: I Became a Chaser	123
Chapter 17: Days Before Going to Denmark	131

STAGE FIVE
Surrender of the Heart
(January 2013-December 2013)

Chapter 18: Arriving in Copenhagen, Denmark	137
Chapter 19: A Magical Dream, Contacting Oskar	141
Chapter 20: The Final Meeting With Oskar	147
Chapter 21: Dark Night of the Soul; Encounter Shela	157
Chapter 22: Gratitude Changes Surrender	161
Chapter 23: The First Healing Session With Shela	169
Chapter 24: Changes From April to August	173
Chapter 25: Second Healing Session with Shela	179
Chapter 26: Important Changes and the Discovery of the Twin Flame	183

Chapter 27: Drum Dance and Spiritual Awakening	191
Chapter 28: Wounds and Thoughts	195
Chapter 29: Goodbye Denmark; See You Next Time!	201

STAGE SIX
Soul's Realization—Becoming Radiant
(January 2014-July 2016)

Chapter 30: What Happened to Santiago in *The Alchemist*?	209
Chapter 31: One Hour Conversation With Oskar	217
Chapter 32: Becoming a Writer	225
Chapter 33: Becoming a Reiki Healer	231
Chapter 34: Becoming a Dancer	239
Chapter 35: What Will Happen Next?	243

STAGE SEVEN
Reunion of the Soul
(July 2016-Present Day)

ABOUT THE COVER

Who created the monkey drawing on the cover and what is the meaning behind it?

Around July 5th, 2009, when my beloved Oskar and I met for the third time, I approached him with excitement and said, "Oskar! You come from Denmark and you said you like drawing and painting very much, right? I like it, too! Would you mind drawing for me something nice in this simple notebook with my colorful pencils? I like inviting inspiring people to draw for me!"

I expected a reply, like, "Oh, sure, my pleasure!" as it was the answer I usually heard from people whom I had invited before. However, Oskar's response was, "Mm... let me think, I don't know if I want to do it or not..."

Just when I was about to feel angry, he suddenly changed his approach and said, "Yes, I would love to! But you need to tell me what you want me to draw for you."

How happy I felt! I asked him to draw me a big monkey and a small Mickey Mouse. That is why the big monkey is wearing a sort of Mickey Mouse hat in the drawing; the chimney on the right side of the cover is a symbol of the P. Loft youth hostel where we met and the number 2009 on the top right represents the year we met.

The drawing remained unfinished, with only these elements on it, until four days later, when we returned from the Cuan Di Xia village (see Chapter One). Oskar then added the green mountain–memories of the Cuan Di Xia village–and the sunflower–my

The Twin Flame Lover of China and Denmark

favorite flower, to the drawing. The pink word on the left bottom of the drawing is in fact the word "rabbit" in graffiti style, because I told him I was born in the year of rabbit. In the burning fire lie our names together: on the top is my nickname DEDE with each letter written both ways—from left to right and from right to left— and on the bottom is the name OSKAR written in the same way. Do you see it?

When Oskar finished the whole drawing and presented it to me, my heart sang; I was simply amazed at his incredible talent and creativity and, most importantly, I felt his LOVE.

Therefore, this is a unique loving drawing made of love, created by my first love—Oskar. I have no reason not to use it as the lovely cover for my first book.

No matter what happens in the future, Oskar will always be the Charming Star Artist of my heart. I believe his innate God given talents and gifts will all blossom and shine in the fullness of time.

Dear Oskar, thank you for the beautiful inspiring drawing. I hope you don't mind that I did not ask your permission, for I simply want to prepare a nice big surprise for you.

PREFACE

A Twin Flame is the other half of our soul who shares the same vibration with us and who matches our energy bodies perfectly. We each have only one twin, known as the ultimate yin or the ultimate yang. It is said that we were split from each other a long, long time ago for the purpose of becoming highly enlightened beings before ascending together to The Source.

Humanity's consciousness has been progressing so much during the last decades that as a result, more and more twin flames are meeting and reuniting with each other. However, due to the rare nature and the overwhelming intensity of this relationship, it can often be misunderstood as weird or even be seen as a catastrophe, as in most cases the two twins come from very different backgrounds and there will be many external differences and difficulties waiting for them to resolve before finally reuniting with each other.

In my experience, a true Twin Flame relationship will always serve as a divine, powerful force to propel both twins to reach the highest possible state of consciousness, which in turn will help them fulfill their mission and transform the planet we live on.

The divine reunion with our twin is believed to be one of the most blissful blessings we can have as a human. In order to make the soul's dream come true, the Great Spirit often sets up many almost impossible obstacles and challenges in our lives, aiming to help us break the false and limited ideas about who we are and what we can achieve. Much soul-level work related to healing and evolving has to occur to prepare both twins to reach a high state of illumination before their final reunion.

Each twin is unique and special, and therefore their storylines and the backgrounds are meant to be different from each other's. However, when it comes to the core center of all Twin Flame relationships, a similar shared dynamic pattern is clearly recognized.

I had the privilege and blessing of meeting my twin Oskar and experiencing the different stages of this very rare relationship from 2009 to 2016. This relationship has completely transformed me and brought many deep and profound changes into my life.

When I heard the inner call to write our story down, I decided to produce this book. I thank you deeply for being my dear reader. By sharing my journey with you, I hope you will find the courage and wisdom within you to pursue your dreams and realize your potential, to wake up to the light to fulfill your soul's mission and live your life beautifully and meaningfully.

The six stages about this relationship that I describe at the beginning of each section describe my personal beliefs based on what I have read and experienced. The purpose of these descriptions is to share and guide the reader, but not to be conclusive; the Twin Flame experience may or may not apply to you.

Know that my spirit is with you.

Love and Light,

Defang Wan
(Indigo DeDe)

ACKNOWLEDGEMENT

One man's accomplishment belongs to all men. Behind this book you are holding there lie many people's contributions. By writing this acknowledgement, I would like to express my deepest appreciation for all the lovely spirits who have guided, uplifted, and enriched my journey.

My loving parents and sister, I thank you for your unconditional love and support. I feel proud of being part of a family with you.

Beijing Double Happiness Courtyard Hotel, I thank you for your trust and for being such a warm and welcoming home for me.

My best friend He Xiaona, no matter where I am and what I do, you always stand by me by sharing your deepest love and trust. What a blessing to have met you at our happy college time!

My Reiki master Begonia, I thank you for teaching me Reiki so that I have become a real healer.

Paulo Coelho, even though I have never met you in person, I thank you deeply for writing those wonderful, inspiring books; I gained so much courage and strength from them.

Dear Ane and Harold, Mette and Thomas, Ova and Inge, Jette, Shela, Benny, Ole, Ellen and Chi, I will always remember and cherish the love we shared in Denmark.

Dear Joanna, I thank you for your excellent editorial talents and all your kind extra support in helping me publish this book. It's truly been a blessing to have met you. I look forward to co-creating my next book with Kora Press.

The Twin Flame Lover of China and Denmark

Dear Wendy, I thank you for being such a wonderful supportive friend, teacher and editor. You are an important supporter within the shadows and are one of the most important forces involved in all I do. You are the source of the light.

Finally and lastly, special thanks to my beloved twin Oskar, for you have made all my dreams come true and helped me become the person I was born to be. You are the brightest shining star in my eye, the most loving angel in my heart, and the most unforgettable rainbow in my soul.

Let only love speak between us.

With blessings,

Defang Wan
(Indigo DeDe)

TWIN FLAME REUNION POEM

Let us release all the pain and sorrow, with joy and honor
together we ascend to heaven.

Let our shadow be banished in infinite light and let us wake up
to our full divinity.

Let us transcend time and space, across mountains and oceans
to emerge into one.

Let you be my God and me be your Goddess; let our soul rejoice
in perfect beauty and harmony.

Let the powerful loving energy of our divine reunion
assist other souls' awakening and transformation.

Let us channel God's words and colors, let His energy
and wisdom flow into our hands and minds;
let us remember our souls' mission and fulfill it
with charm and grace.

Let us invite the sun, the moon, the spirit, the masters, stars,
flowers, birds and all loving beings to our sacred celebration; let us
sing and dance in the eternal truth of our soul.

In ecstasy we heal the world with Absolute Love.

BRIEF INTRODUCTION

This is a true story of the writer–Defang Wan (Indigo DeDe).

In 2009, in a youth hostel in Beijing, she met a Danish boy named Oskar. The very moment she saw his face, she "recognized" him immediately. She thought to herself: "Aha! I have met him before! He is the Special One I've been waiting for for a long, long time!"

The great joy, the beauty of it, the color of it, the wonder of it, made her want to fly up to the sky to have a celebration with everyone! However, Destiny whispered: "Be prepared, the final test of your soul is about to begin..."

A path pre-designed by the Higher Intelligence awaited her. She began to awake by asking, "Who am I? What am I here to do? Where did I originally come from? What is Reality? Is it possible to reshape it? How can I change my destiny?"

In 2013, she made her way to Denmark, in search of her dream and love. From this moment on, the whole story began to take on an unbelievably mysterious turn... How was her life in Denmark? What did the Danish healer say to her? The very Special One–Oskar–was he the other half of her soul? Did she manage to wake up to her higher powers and potential? How did she finally heal and transform herself? In the end, did she find her life path and was she able to follow it?

From 2009 to 2016, from Beijing to Denmark, from the little self to the higher self, from darkness to light, from being lost to awakening, this book is telling you:

The Twin Flame Lover of China and Denmark

> A deeply touching love story between
> the two halves of one soul;
> A magical destiny-transforming journey
> from Beijing to Denmark;
> A story of a woman who is dedicated to looking
> for the meaning of life;
> A profound path of search toward
> the fulfillment of one's divine mission.

STAGE ONE

Recognition—
Love in Heaven

(July 2009-February 2010)

*A*t this stage, everything is beautiful and perfect. Twins exist in a completely harmonious and blissful dimension made of pure love and joy. It might look like just another common love story. However, beyond the surface, a deeper level of awakening and energetic preparation is simultaneously happening... The meeting is meant to be for their intended higher purpose and divine mission...

Chapter 1

Love—Recognition of the Soul

Having got a job as receptionist at the P. Loft Youth Hostel in Beijing, I had been sublimely happy, feeling lively and full of energy. This lasted for three months. Then suddenly and unexpectedly, for a few days I had a very strange "empty feeling" in my heart. I seemed to have lost all interest in my surroundings, which included flowers and even the people I interacted with. The lively noise and activities around me didn't seem to hold my attention any more; I no longer felt the passion or excitement they had previously inspired in me.

Then one day, as I looked at our lobby, I noticed there were a few Chinese people and westerners there, busy with various activities–having fun, talking to each other. Before, I had looked at them with a fresh feeling, feeling that they were all connected with me, that we were "friends" to some extent. But now each and every one of them just seemed so ordinary to me, having absolutely no connection with me.

"Where is that Special One? Why hasn't he showed up yet? Where can he be?" Thinking about these strange questions, my heart was filled with a feeling of loss, which I had never experienced before. The previous strange "empty feeling" flooded back into me.

"Where exactly is that Special One?" I kept asking myself. For the first time in my life, my heart strongly desired to meet that "Special One." Using all my will power, my hands wrote in my notebook: "Love, where is love? Come... come to me..." Having written it down, I half forgot about it; everything seemed to return to normal.

The Twin Flame Lover of China and Denmark

Three days later, on a sunny afternoon, two guests arrived at my reception: two young western backpackers. One of them was just some stranger; he didn't really hold my attention after the first look. But the second one... Aha! My soul received a huge shock. I "recognized" you! I heard myself thinking, "This face, how familiar. I've seen it somewhere before! This person, how special! I've met him before! He is going to play a very special and important role in my life; we are going to have a very, very special relationship..."

I remember my heart immediately became so happy and so excited; it seemed as if you were emanating a powerful energy, directed straight at me.

Before meeting him, I had often imagined or created a fantasy of meeting the "Special One;" I had thought about *him* countless times... I couldn't predict how *he* would look, or how *he* would appear in my life, but I knew I had been unconsciously waiting for *him*. The moment I saw him, I knew: "You are the Special One!"

This magical "recognition" lasted for only a few seconds in my mind. As a receptionist, I acted as if nothing had happened, pretending everything was just normal.Following a huge shock, I then became involved in the standard "reception procedure." I started to copy your passport, initiated the check-in process, etc.

You acted quite normal during our first meeting; you didn't really say much, looking at this and that, not looking at me... a little bit shy, or rather, quite reserved. Following the direction of your glance, it seemed as though I didn't stand out for you. But that did not really matter because quite soon, you also recognized me.

I looked at your passport information with joy and excitement, thinking, "So, you come from Denmark–the beautiful fairy tale country! Your name is Oskar! I like this name, it feels special to me! You were born in the year 1985, you are two years older than me. It is fortunate that you are not two years younger than me! I don't like the idea of my 'Special One' being younger than me. You were born in the capital city of Denmark–Copenhagen... you are about 1.76cm tall."

After the check-in process was completed, I joyfully took you to the eight-people dormitory you had reserved. On the way, I gave you a very detailed introduction, explaining about our bar and our hostel. I probably said more than was required of me, much more than I would normally do. I also purposefully chose the longer way to go to your dormitory. I slowed down my normally fast speaking speed, and added more unnecessary English words. All because I wanted to stay a little bit longer with you, observe you, or rather, secretly adore you for few more seconds.

I can't remember what exactly I did say, but I felt as if I was walking on a beautiful rainbow-colored cloud. It was a feeling of floating... How happy I was! The never-before felt joy felt like it would fly me up to the sky! I wished I could just jump into your arms immediately, touch you, hug you, kiss you, and eat you up!

After coming back to the reception, I stared at the copy of your passport once again, absorbing all the information it contained. There were lots of colorful fireworks setting off in my heart! When I sat down, I wanted to stand up; when I stood up, I wanted to sit down. So I kept myself running around the small chair in my reception, wanting to jump for joy! Wanting to celebrate! Joy! Joy beyond any measure! Infinite joy! I felt as if there was high electricity flowing through me. I wanted to dance, to hug everyone I knew. I wanted to happily tell them, "Look! I finally met him! I have waited for him and now at last I have seen him!!! "

I thought, "Yes, you are different from the other westerners! The others are friends, friends I can hang out with, talk to, and have fun with. But you are not a friend, you are the Special One! You seemed quite shy and reserved, you didn't talk very much. But I always like talking and communicating with people, and I am especially good at making friends with backpackers. I am open-minded, passionate and sincere. To some extent, I really think I am popular among foreign travelers. So, I believed it would not be difficult for me to get close to you, with the purpose of attracting your attention. I think I am a very loving person. So, I might have some sort of magical chance.

"Oh no! Judging from the direction of your glance, you didn't seem to feel that I was 'special'... This situation is beginning to feel rather difficult... Oh my God! Please don't tell me that by the time you check out of this hostel you won't even have noticed my name. From the beginning to the end of your stay, there could not have been anyone other than me who felt so excited, so joyful, so much wanting to...? Well... well... I'd better be normal, be a little reserved, wait and see how things go for the next few days, follow the natural flow... Anyway, you are just a traveler, only booked into the hostel for seven or eight nights here; after that, you will leave and check out, like many other of my backpacker friends... But I am really very, very happy that you have come here!"

For the first two days, I hardly saw you. I was feeling quite frustrated and upset, even rather angry with myself. Annoyed, I thought, "Damn! I have recognized you, but you haven't recognized me! Or else, how could it be that two days have passed, but you haven't even looked for me to have a chat? Maybe you won't like me or find that I am special or adorable, maybe nothing is going to happen between us... Well... well... So be it. You are just a traveler passing through, you are going to leave here anyway. Perhaps it's better that nothing happens. Quietly come, quietly go, leave nothing!

"But no! You are the Special One! It's not that easy for me to have finally met you. Should I just watch you leave, let you go with my eyes wide open, without doing or saying anything? No...! Why didn't you look for me to have a small talk with me? Perhaps I am just being insane? Or crazy? The previous 'recognition' was just something stupid? Idiotic? Or what?"

When I thought that you were still here, you were living here, my heart began to beat strongly, you seemed to draw me to you like a magnet. I came to our hostel's lobby more and more often, only because I wanted to see if you were there or not. I often searched for

The Twin Flame Lover of China and Denmark

you in the crowds of western foreigners in P. Loft. I simply wanted so much to see you, to be close to you, to talk to you, to be with you!

One day, I saw you standing alone in our lobby. My heart immediately started to beat quickly, electricity started to flow! I wasn't deterred by the idea of what others might think. Instead, I bravely walked straight up to you! No, not to you, but to the whole world, the whole universe! My heart was beating happily!

It was our first real conversation since your arrival. In order to avoid any suggestion of "I really like you, I really want to know more about you," I deliberately asked questions that a receptionist might legitimately ask, such as, "Where are you from? Why did you come to China? What do you do? What do you like to do in your free time? What do your parents do? Do you have any brothers or sisters? How old are you? How do you feel about our hostel? Are you enjoying your stay here? Where are you going next?..." These kind of questions that I had asked so many times of so many different people, in most cases out of sheer curiosity or sometimes, just out of duty or trying to be polite. It was only in your case that those questions were asked out of a passionate interest. They were messages of love!

When I was talking to you, time and space only existed between us; everything around us could no longer be seen or heard any more. I could only see you, and your lovely eyes, they were special enough to make my heart tingle. Time didn't feel like it was as dense and boring as cement any more; in a blink, it was magically transformed into a beautiful flower, which felt so loving, and unbelievable...

After this initial conversation, we seemed to want to talk with each other again, see each other again and again. Once it started, neither of us wanted it to stop. It seemed as if a natural, invisible, powerful force of attraction existed between us, which made us want to find all kinds of excuses to meet again... I wanted to help you find some graffiti spray, to see you again tomorrow, to be with you...

You told me you started to draw when you were five years old, you liked drawing and painting very much, you wanted to become a very good artist. You didn't need to be very famous, but you would prefer your name to be known by at least some people who know and understand what art really is. Currently, you were studying at an art school located in Odense—where the famous writer Hans Christian Andersen was born.

I told you Andersen was very famous in China; almost every Chinese citizen knows who he is. I had read some of his famous fairy tales in my primary school. And that was the only thing I knew about Denmark.

I asked you what exactly Andersen had looked like. You told me that he had quite a strange face, with a very big nose. It was hard for me to imagine what he really looked like. So I changed the subject. I asked you why you chose P. Loft to stay at. You laughed a little, saying, "Because your price is the best on the Internet!"

On hearing this, I thought, "It's lucky the first hostel I had applied to—Peking International Hostel—had not hired me. Their price is really very expensive; a student, or rather a backpacker like you, would never go there! What brought me to Beijing and to P. Loft? Were we destined to meet here? Is this so-called destiny?"

One time, I told you there was a very lovely park, close to our hostel, where there were lots of trees and flowers, plus a very special wooden building. I deliberately asked you by using a very relaxed voice: "Would you like to go there with me to have a look? It's one of my favorite places in Beijing."

You said yes, and there we went, with our secretly happy hearts.

So, I took you to the wooden building located in the park. From there, we spent time watching the busy Second Ring Road in Beijing. I didn't know what you were really thinking or seeing, but I stole a few secret glances at your face every few seconds, thinking, "How come you are so beautiful, unique, handsome, loving and warm? And you are speaking to my heart! Your energy, every piece of your energy, how could they appear so special, so attractive to me? How wonderful life is! Do you secretly adore me, too? Is there any possibility that you are already starting to like me? Have you discovered that I am actually quite special, too? I seemed to be sensing something... after all, if you don't like me, why did you draw for me? Why did you eat rice, watermelon, green-tea flavored ice cream with me? Why did you go out with me? You are not that kind of person who would just go out with anyone..."

One minute I would want to maintain my fantasy. The next minute I was urging myself to be more realistic. I was just an ordinary person without any special attraction. Whereas he was so beautiful and special, how could he possibly be interested in me? Until now, all his words and actions had been quite normal, with no indication that something special was going on! I was in the grip of a fantasy, thinking that someone special like him could fall in love with the ordinary DeDe... the possibility was really too small...

"But maybe, like me, he is hiding his feelings? Now I am almost struggling with myself... Does he like me or not??"

In the evening of that same day, I just "happened" to meet you again in our lobby. You told me you wanted to go to the 798 art district the following day, and asked me how you could get there. As usual, I explained the route in as much detail as possible, afraid that you would get lost and confused somewhere.

While I was talking to you, I was thinking to myself, "Would you like to invite me to go to District 798 with you tomorrow? I would like to do that very much. I am off for the next two days, and you only have two or three days left here..."

Having completed my explanations, the professional receptionist should have said, "Goodbye, see you tomorrow. I hope you have a wonderful day there, enjoy!" Just before I turned to go, you asked me, "Would you like to go there with me tomorrow? Are you available?"

At that moment lots of beautiful flowers were blooming in my heart! Happily I replied, "I am not working for the next two days. I have never been to the 798 art district, which I think must be very

The Twin Flame Lover of China and Denmark

interesting! See you tomorrow at 9 a.m. at the reception!!"

I couldn't really find any effective way to fall asleep that night, because I was so full of excitement and joy. I gazed at the beautiful stars in the sky; they too seemed to be feeling happy for me!

The day we visited District 798, you sprayed a lot of creative graffiti on the walls there. You were obviously excited and happy, and so was I! It was the first time I had seen how graffiti were created, so I felt quite inspired and interested. You were focused while you were in your creative mood and I felt you were just so special and charming. This reinforced my feeling that you too were a great piece of art!

After coming back to P. Loft, I proudly and loudly praised your wonderful painting talent in front of my boss. After getting his approval, we decided to paint a big Mickey Mouse image on the wall of P. Loft. Why Mickey Mouse? Because he's my favorite cartoon character and I had a special fondness for him. And, to some extent, I thought you looked very much like Mickey Mouse!

Your expression suggested that you didn't know whether to laugh or cry. You said, "Okay... but I'm not sure I like the idea of looking like Mickey Mouse..."

Let's forget about Mickey Mouse. What I really wanted to tell you was, "You and Mickey Mouse are both special and lovely! I like you both a lot!"

In the late afternoon you successfully painted a beautiful Mickey Mouse on the wall of P. Loft for me. It was very creative and very lovely; I couldn't have loved it more. At one point you were looking for a specific bottle of spray paint among many, but you just couldn't find it. I asked you what color you wanted, and you told me. Then, magically, I saw it. With the speed of light, I picked it up and gave it to you. You thanked me gently and softly, looking at me, with eyes full of tenderness and love!

I almost fainted! My heart beat wildly! "Please," I thought, "don't tell me that he has already fallen in love with me! What did his glance mean? Why are there deep and touching messages of love flowing from his eyes into mine? This is TOO beautiful!" I could hardly bear it!

Afterwards, the two of us went to Hou Hai Lake by bike. It's a place you must see if you are exploring Beijing. But the bars and the noise there really didn't attract us. It was not the kind of attraction that appealed to us. So we decided to ride back after a short while.

However, it suddenly started to rain, quite heavily. We couldn't ride our bikes so we followed the crowd to a place where many people were sheltering from the rain.

Strangely, one empty chair was available, even though so many people were standing under the shelter. Out of politeness, I asked you to take that seat. You insisted I should sit down. I thought that since you had come from a small country, whereas I came from a very big one, it meant that *I* should take good care of *you*, rather than vice versa. So I insisted you should sit down!

Finally, you sat down on the chair. Instantly, you said something like, "We can sit together, I can hold you." While you were saying it, you were also making an encouraging gesture. Then, you looked at me very gently, waiting for my reply.

I looked at you; your eyes looked so gentle and soft, loving and sincere. It was the light of adoration. Yes, I saw it! My heart raced and emanated high voltage electricity, which was flowing all around me. I just couldn't believe what was happening. I thought, "This kind of 'sit together on the same chair' invitation wouldn't be extended to a friend, would it? What does this mean exactly? Does it imply that he likes me? Is it fondness? Adoration? I am really so excited, nervous, happy! Something completely out of my expectation!"

There were many people around us; a few of them cast occasional glances at us. I remember one girl, who seemed to understand what was really going on between you and me. Her eyes were full of curiosity, maybe she was wondering: "This is rather interesting! Will she sit down or not... ?"

Yes! Of course I would sit down! Of course I would grasp at the chance of love! I sat down with my love, letting him hold me. I was extremely happy, joyful and excited, my heart beating fast.

After a few seconds, I thought, "Wait a minute! Foreigners are said to be very open! They can hug anyone, everyone! They would even kiss their own dog, or any pets they might have! Maybe this gesture is just a friendly gesture? But no! The eyes cannot hide what the heart feels! What I felt was a sincere, gentle, sweet message of LOVE! It was a surprisingly sudden feeling of joy! Have you really fallen in love with me?

This was our first intimate experience.

Quite soon, we were following the crowd, running in the rain. Running... running... then, suddenly, we were holding hands. My brain became totally blank; I was speechless. "Am I just dreaming?!"

I wasn't dreaming. This was really happening. We were holding hands! I wasn't the only one who was in LOVE! You, too, had fallen in love with me within seven days!

By the time we got back to P. Loft, it was already quite late. We said that we would meet at reception early the following morning, and then go to a very interesting village called Cuan Di Xia in a suburb of Beijing. A few days earlier I had asked you if you were interested in going there with me. You had said yes. See, it was my idea again! I really wanted very much to get you there, but to do what? Because the day after tomorrow, you would be checking out. I simply wanted to go to a very lovely and special place with you, have a beautiful memory, as our special "souvenir" of each other.

Next morning you checked out, stored your luggage at our reception, told my co-worker that you would be back on the second day. After that, we happily headed on our way to Cuan Di Xia.

While we were waiting for the long distance bus at the bus station, many drivers approached us, trying to persuade us to hire their small minivan. No, we didn't want that, and we felt a little bit annoyed by them. So, two of us walked away from the crowd.

The Twin Flame Lover of China and Denmark

Walking... walking... All of a sudden, our hands found each other again, sweetly, firmly....

Everything around us, the people, the sky, the road, the birds, the summer sun, the flowers, the breeze... all were melting in LOVE.

"I have never held hands with any boys before; you are the first one, the Special One." Hearing that, you were quite surprised, feeling lucky, or rather, feeling special.

All the way, on the bus, we held hands; the flower of love blossomed.

We liked Cuan Di Xia village very much; we liked the big mountains, the old green trees, and the honest people who live there. We found a lovely family hotel to check into, and then we happily went out to climb the mountain.

We enjoyed being together. So many times, I wished you would kiss me or at least ask my permission if you could. But no, you didn't ask! I wasn't angry at all, just a little disappointed. I was just wondering, "According to some movies or my own expectations, now is a very good time to let a kiss happen, right? But why hasn't he asked me yet?"

We went back to the family hotel we had chosen. As we were sitting on the roof of the house, we could clearly see the big mountains right in front of us and the many beautiful shining stars up above us. What a lovely night it was! And my beloved, sitting right next to me!

All of a sudden, you startled me by asking, "Can I kiss you?" All I could feel was great happiness, joy, excitement and a little shyness. My blushing face turned away from you, you couldn't see the emotions that were playing havoc with me. I thought, "This is going to be my first kiss! I've never kissed anyone before, so I don't know how to kiss! But you are the Special One I have been waiting for! I have saved my first kiss for you! I don't want to kiss anyone except you! So, come and kiss me!"

I gently said, "Yes..!"

It was already 10 or 11 p.m.; we needed to go to bed. We chose

The Twin Flame Lover of China and Denmark

one of the four or five beds in our room. Initial hesitation was soon replaced by our sweet hugs and loving kisses. Our shyness and inexperience meant that we were still fully clothed. But in the middle of the night you suddenly woke up and said something like, "I'm sorry, but do you mind if Mickey Mouse now takes off his long trousers? I have my short pants on; I've never been to bed in my long trousers before."

We laughed together—the ice was broken. The hugging and kissing continued. It was a magical night. We both experienced a MYSTERIOUS BEAUTY beyond words. Perhaps our souls were embracing each other as well. Otherwise, how could it be so wonderful?

My first love, sweet as vanilla, beautiful as roses, lovely as sunflowers, and shining like stars, started in this way.

What was awaiting us in the future? And how did I, a girl from a small farming family in a faraway province, come to be working as an English-speaking receptionist in a youth hostel in Beijing?

Chapter 2

English, the Magical Beginning of Everything

I started to learn English when I was eleven years old in first grade of middle school. My first impression of this language was that it felt interesting and fresh; I felt very curious and joyful about it; it seemed as if English was "talking" or "calling" to me; it was so easy and so natural for me to understand, as if English and I knew each other well.

From middle school to high school, for six whole years, while the other subjects always made me feel thick-headed and stupid, English was the one which made me feel worthy and clever; it made me think that I possessed some talent. English was my favorite class, the one that lit up my whole world and being.

When I was about to go to college, I confidently chose International Business and Trade as my major. I thought, "There must be lots of English lessons for students who take this major; the teachers must be teaching English to a very high standard. I can make good use of their skills by learning English well and speaking fluently! Moreover, after graduation I will be qualified to find a job in international business or international trade. This will bring me the opportunity to speak English with westerners, to engage in business style communication with them. I will be able to practice English with them face to face and even have the opportunity to get in touch with the western culture! That really sounds very interesting and attractive!"

So the decision was made.

The Twin Flame Lover of China and Denmark

My three years of college life were extremely happy and fulfilling, mainly because I put almost all my time and energy into studying English. Every week I would go to a place called "The English Corner" in other universities to practice my oral English with other students. I would study very hard and passionately for all my English exams; I took part in the English Speech Contest and in English Salon activities. I would listen and learn to sing many English songs; I would memorize many new English words. I would make friends with students who also liked to speak English. Anything and everything that was English-related would immediately light up my whole world.

Other students told me they had the following reasons for learning English: "My parents want me to learn English; they plan to send me to a college in the USA or England, so I have to learn, even though I don't really like it or feel any passion about it."

"I learn it, because it will help me get very high scores in my examination. It will be good for my MBA degree."

"I learn it because I want to have a western boyfriend; I am quite interested in western culture and am hoping to find romance with someone who speaks English."

"I learn it because almost everyone around me is learning it."

What was my motivation? Joy! Pure joy, the kind of joy and happiness that colored my every waking moment. I had no idea that underneath the joy and passion lay the magic, a destiny, a dream fulfilled and love...

After graduating I easily found a job as an "English-speaking sales representative," selling American products to American people on the phone.

Initially I felt that my job was very interesting, exciting, or even challenging—for the first time in my life, I could speak English with foreigners on the phone. It was a thrilling experience!

However, I soon became depressed by the people who didn't want to buy, who asked to be removed from our calling list and treated me as a nuisance. I realized that I didn't want to speak English merely to earn a commission on a sale. My self-esteem and confidence sank to zero and I felt completely demoralized.

I had to get a different job to restore my self-confidence and be able to give some support to my parents, who had supported me for so many years.

I accepted a second job, sending promotional emails to potential clients. However, I soon found that it bored me, and I started to hate the job. I felt nothing in common with my co-workers.

Just when I felt I had sunk to rock bottom, a friend in Beijing contacted me. She was working as an English-speaking receptionist in an international youth hostel. She felt that I would enjoy a similar situation, which would enable me to talk in English with guests from all over the world.

The more I discovered about similar youth hostels, the more excited I became. The management required the staff to speak English well, to be able to talk easily with foreigners and have an outgoing personality.

Such a job would be perfect for me. On the other hand, I had never been to Beijing and knew nobody there, except for this one friend.

I went home for a while to weigh up the idea. Eventually I felt that God's will was leading my heart and guiding me to overcome my misgivings, setting me on the right path.

I narrowed down the possibilities to two youth hostels in Beijing, contacted them and arranged interviews.

During the 16-hour train journey to Beijing I worried about the possibility of failing both interviews and being stranded in Beijing, without even the means to return home.

Indeed, the first interview did not go well and I received a cold, "We'll let you know" outcome.

I walked the crowded streets, as fear crawled over me. Eventually I forced myself to think positive thoughts, in anticipation of the

The Twin Flame Lover of China and Denmark

second interview.

When I arrived at P. Loft International Youth Hostel I was immediately enchanted: murals on the wall, green bamboo, a spring flowing in the courtyard and a large and strange barrel. I felt energy everywhere; it appeared to be fresh and exotic. My spirits soared.

I felt great joy and excitement. As I went from their front door to the lobby, I saw the authentic wooden chairs and tables and the Tibetan style pictures hanging on the wall. More joy started to flood into my heart, which was happily singing, "Wow! Wow! This is 'love at first sight'! I feel a very strong and intense sense of belonging in this place; I like it a lot. It would be really great if I could stay and work here!" I felt very optimistic about being taken on.

Perhaps this time, God's will and my human heart's desire would align perfectly. My interview went well. How lucky I was! I was hired! They even told me that I could move into their employees' dormitory that afternoon.

Can you imagine how happy and how grateful I felt at that moment?! All of a sudden, I went from having nothing to having everything. I would have free food, free accommodation, and a lovely job, which would soon provide me with tons of opportunities to speak English with western foreigners! In this super lovely place called heaven! Wow! I was really so, so happy! My worry and anxiety finally disappeared. It was beginner's luck.

I was given about seven days to get familiar with my duties. During that period I worked hard and learned a lot, applying my heart and soul. I told myself that I had to cherish this precious opportunity, and learn to be a responsible person. So yes, everything from small to big was written down carefully in my notebook, to ensure I remembered my lessons well. I wanted to start working on my own as soon as possible, instead of needing supervision by experienced co-workers. In other words, I wanted to enjoy total freedom and total independence, to be my own boss.

On the sixth day, I started to work on my own at reception. I was feeling a little bit nervous, worried that I might make mistakes; at the same time I was feeling great joy and excitement to finally become independent. I knew that an important time of my life had just arrived!

I remember that for the next few months, almost every day, life felt so happy, fresh, free, funny, interesting, lovely, wonderful, colorful, great, beautiful, and excellent. I felt that life had finally, generously, opened a door for me, showing me a fantastic world made of colors and wonders! This was the world I had been longing for, while I was working in Guangzhou. My dream had come true!

I liked the creativity, authenticity, uniqueness, and wonders of P. Loft! I liked the purple grape trellis, the blooming flowers, the green bamboos, the two lovely swings, the special bells, the graffiti zone, the loft style basketball court and the bar. I liked the liveliness and colors introduced by so many different types of people. I liked seeing and meeting all of them! They would sing, dance, draw, play guitar, play chess, play basketball, talk, drink, fall in love, practice Tai Chi, sit under the sun, read, go for a walk, do nothing, be positive, negative, crazy, absurd, wild, ambitious, normal, abnormal... What a lively world! What a lovely P. Loft!

I reveled in meeting so many young backpackers from all over the world. They always had a very big and heavy backpack on their back, and they all said they were traveling to Shanghai, Xi'an, Cheng Du, India, Nepal... I felt that they were so free and so courageous! They were very exotic and interesting foreigners! They, in turn, appreciated me, whom they perceived as being full of color and energy. So of course we hung out together.

We had lovely walks in Beijing's small alleys *(huttings)*, where we ate many delicious local foods (hot pot, ice cream, small steamed buns, etc.); we went to Hou Hai and the Summer Palace, hired a boat and enjoyed the rides on the beautiful lakes there. We sat together, talked about lots of interesting topics, humorously and passionately. We went out in the evenings and enjoyed ourselves, climbing up apple trees and picking apples. We painted together on the wall of P. Loft, freely and creatively; we talked frankly about ourselves, about this and that, about western and eastern traditions and customs...

What about my receptionist job? It couldn't have been more fun. So often, my small reception area would be crowded with people! People who were checking in, checking out, storing their luggage, asking for directions to the subway, booking trips to the Great Wall or a Kung Fu show, buying train tickets, paying for their rooms, saying "Hi" to me, waiting for me, asking for help, inviting me for dinner or going somewhere, asking for a tooth brush, toothpaste, towels, a quilt, slippers, shampoo, a kettle, an air-conditioning controller...

I was so busy, so useful, so needed, so welcomed. I felt so excited, so thrilled, so wonderful. There were so many people waiting for me, needing me. More importantly, at the same time I could practice English in real practical situations. Wow! My youthful dream about speaking English with western foreigners was finally fully fulfilled! I couldn't be more satisfied than this! It had just totally gone beyond all my secret expectations! WOW!

I had finally found a place custom made for me, a heaven in which I could not only freely and happily demonstrate who I was, what I liked to do, what I was good at, but also I could practice English with many foreigners, broaden my cultural horizon and observe a wonderful world made up of freedom and world travelers. Life—you are just too beautiful! My life as a receptionist, I was loving it!

Chapter 3

Love Stayed, Love Left

We came back to P. Loft from Cuan Di Xia village the very next day. A train ticket you had booked a few days earlier had arrived. That night, around 10 p.m., you would be heading to your next travel destination—the city of Ping Yao. It seemed as if separation was inevitable.

Separation? No, it was not something we expected or were ready for. Even though it was something we should have known from the very beginning that it would soon be upon us!

Our facial expressions remained peaceful and we pretended nothing was wrong. But deep down, we were saddened and concerned. We didn't really know how to deal with it.

I suddenly felt anger toward you and toward cruel destiny. I thought, "But last night our souls were hugging each other so sweetly, and now we have to separate? Will I see you again in this lifetime? Things are happening too fast and too suddenly! You are leaving too soon! I don't know how to handle this!"

At that moment, all I wanted to do was to run away, run away from you and my restless emotions, and then, to find a safe place to hide.

Therefore, I was a little cold when I told you that I needed to go back to my own dormitory to take a shower and wash my clothes. I even said that I didn't know when I would be back, but I definitely would say goodbye to you before you left.

My words left you feeling rather cheerless. You thought in silence for few seconds and then gently said that you would be waiting for

The Twin Flame Lover of China and Denmark

me in the lobby.

Around 8 p.m. I came back to reception, ready to work my night shift. However, I couldn't help anxiously thinking, "In two hours he will be leaving! How will I feel at that moment? Do I really want him to leave? No! I am not prepared for him to leave yet! I can't accept it! I don't know how to face it!"

You had been waiting for me in the lobby and you noticed when I arrived, so you walked into my reception area a few minutes later. I was talking with my co-worker about our changing shift stuff at that time. You politely interrupted us by saying to my co-worker, "Excuse me, Susan, I really have something very important to talk to DeDe about. Can you please give us a few minutes...?"

Susan already knew about our feelings for each other, so she left with an understanding sweet smile.

I admired your courage and directness; I appreciated your love. But still, I didn't know what to do or what to say.

For the first time, I saw sadness in your eyes. You were feeling low. Yes, I could clearly feel your feelings, as if they were my own. I wondered what you would say—goodbye, or what?

You cleared your throat and gathered your courage; you then said that you had been thinking for quite a long time and you realized that you didn't want us to separate, didn't want to leave me. You wanted to stay for one more week! You asked if I would like you to stay and suggested we went to the train station together to return your ticket.

I was shocked by your decision. It was something I never expected or imagined. My mind went totally blank and I was speechless for a long time. I can't say I was not feeling happy after hearing your words, but many different voices arguing in my head made me feel very unsettled.

I heard them saying, "No! Don't let him stay! Let him leave! You two don't have a future! He is from Denmark and you are from China, this love is too unrealistic and impossible! Don't let yourself get hurt or disappointed by this kind of relationship! Let him go!

The Twin Flame Lover of China and Denmark

You have already met him and shared the most beautiful love with him. This is enough, more than enough. Let it be, let its beauty and mystery remain unspoiled in their own time and space. Cherish it, bury it, and think of it as time goes by. But never try to think of any possibility of developing it! It's dangerous...

"It could be dangerous, very dangerous! There are many aspects of you that you don't want him to know. You don't like those parts of yourself and you know that once they get discovered, he will definitely leave you and conclude that you are an ugly person who is not worthy of his love and affection. Therefore, it's better to finish this love right now, when you are still being cherished as the Beautiful One, instead of being loathed as the wrongly chosen one some day in the future.

"But wait a minute! I really like him so much! He is the Special One I have been waiting for for such a long time! Should I really just let him go like this? We're just getting to know each other! Maybe something will happen if I let him stay? I secretly want him to stay! He is truly very lovely and adorable; I like him a LOT! Even though it's only been seven days, I feel we've known each other for a long time. I can't let this special wonderful intimacy disappear from my life so quickly! No no, I can't, I don't want to!

"But what about the future? What are you going to do in the long term? Long distance love is, after all, impossibly difficult love..."

My doubts and fears were much bigger than my hope and joy. Therefore, lowering my voice, I quietly said to you, "I don't really know. This is your decision. Whatever you decide will be very important to both of us. So please, you decide."

Because you didn't receive a positive or supportive reply from me, your mood became gray, you told me that you would think it through. I felt even more unsettled.

Shortly afterwards you came back, full of joy and excitement. You declared that you had thoroughly thought it through and that you wanted very much to stay!

The Twin Flame Lover of China and Denmark

Feelings of great joy and excitement, as well as worries and fears, overwhelmed me. My emotions had never been as complicated and strange as that before.

After asking my co-worker Susan to take my shift for a while, we took the subway to the train station to return your ticket. On the way, you whispered, "DeDe, look, I noticed the man sitting over there has been using his subway card to clean his nails. I think it's quite odd and interesting. Don't you think?"

Yes, I agreed. But what was truly strange and funny was the fact that you noticed it. "Dear Oskar! You are weird! One of a kind! But I like it!" I couldn't help laughing out loud.

We successfully got the refund for your ticket. You were happy and excited; you retrieved your stored luggage and extended your stay at the hostel.

I was on my night shift that night and you were there with me for a few hours. We were chatting and talking like old friends. You told me that when you were about 14 years old, you and your friends had very long hair—your special way of expressing your great fondness for the Beatles. But all of you were very lazy, so lazy that you would leave your hair unwashed for weeks. And then, one day, you and your friends were horrified to discover that there were some "small animals" living in your hair!

Your funny expressions, especially your personalized "small animals" made me burst out laughing. I thought to myself, "Oskar! You are really something! You are very expressive and creative! I like it!"

You told me that Denmark's summers were quite cool, never as hot as Beijing. In Denmark, you would wear long jeans instead of shorts.

Hearing that, I wanted so much to see how you would look with your long jeans on! At my request, you went to your room and put your jeans on.

I looked at you with eyes full of love and light and used the word "beautiful" to compliment you. That felt rather odd to you, but you were so happy and excited, that you even danced around happily to the lovely song, *Here Comes the Sun* by the Beatles as background music.

You could not imagine, how much I loved your precious playfulness and child-like innocence!

The following week, we went to a beautiful mountain, to a valley, a forest, and the Great Wall of China. Our love and our beating hearts were witnessed by the sun, the moon, the blooming flowers, the flying birds and the passers-by.

I remember, you would often jump around me happily, inspired by your heart's joy and love. And then, you would take my hands lovingly, smiling, full of tenderness and sincerity.

Being with you, it felt so natural, so fresh, so interesting, so funny, so sincere, so true, so beautiful, so joyful, so unforgettable, so intimate, so familiar, with "no need to talk," as if we had known and been with each other for a long, long time. Many times, I could not help thinking that I must be the luckiest person in the world. And I wondered why God had decided to give this sort of golden blessing to ordinary me.

My previous worries and fears had all totally gone, replaced by the realization that love can grow ever sweeter and shine even more. I was so happy that you had stayed!

The week went by so quickly. Both of us thought it was time for you to travel somewhere else in China, to experience a different place and culture. In the end, you chose the city of Urumqi and you said that you would be back within a few days. You said that three or four days later you would catch your flight to India and stay there for about one month, according to your original travel plan.

We went to the train station together. Before you got on the train, we kissed goodbye. Then you passionately commented, "Wow, that kiss was a really very good one, a successful kiss!"

Again, I burst out laughing, once more adoring your unique

The Twin Flame Lover of China and Denmark

loveliness and weirdness.

As I went back to P. Loft alone, a feeling of loss immediately enveloped me. I realized it was all because you had left. I started to miss you, and think about you.

The following day I was working alone at the reception. I tried to pretend nothing was wrong. However, I just couldn't control my emotions any more. I ran to the courtyard and started to cry. I was crying like a child and I heard the inner child saying, "I miss my Oskar, I miss him very much, I feel as if I have lost a part of myself... I want him back!"

Just when I finished crying, I heard my phone ringing at reception. I quickly dried my tears and ran to pick up the phone.

Darling, it was you! You were calling me from Urumqi! How surprised I was! How delighted I was! What a magical coincidence! When I was crying, you were calling!

You asked how I was feeling and what I had been doing. I put aside my shyness and told you directly that I had been missing you very much. You said you, too, had never missed anyone like this before. My heart smiled, wishing you would come back soon.

About three days later, you came back. I went to the train station to pick you up. We were seeing each other again! We hugged and kissed, our hearts rejoiced. But at the same time, I started to think about your leaving.

I thought, "In a few days' time, he is leaving for India and will stay there for one month. And then, he will go back to his country— Denmark. And then? Is there any 'then'? Are we going to see each other again? Does such an impossible opportunity really exist??

"No no... I had better be realistic and wake up to reality. The truth is that of course we won't see each other again! Of course there is no possibility of continuing our relationship! There is no point! In order to avoid the pain and suffering, I had better cut away this emotional attachment before I get involved too deeply. I will not tell him my email address and I will change my phone number, so that there is no way for him to contact me, so that we won't talk or think about each other.

"Yes, this is the right way to do it. Even though it feels painful, it is wise. I will wait for the best moment to explain this to him, not now, not tomorrow, but perhaps one or two days before he leaves."

We had joy, we had fun, we had love. But still, we had to say goodbye. The day before our last, I told you about my decision and suggested that we should not contact each other after your departure.

I cannot remember what exactly you said but I clearly felt you were sad and dispirited. Afterwards, you stopped talking to me, and kept walking in silence.

For the first time, the beautiful and harmonious energy field between us was distorted by an interference.

I could feel your suffering and pain, which made me feel sorry and guilty. I never wanted to cause you sorrow or sadness. So I started to question myself, "Why did I say those stupid words to hurt him? Why did I lie to myself? I like him so much, I want him to be happy and smile! Did I make the wrong decision? Should I take back those lies and speak out the truth?"

A long time went by, then I broke the silence by asking why you didn't want to speak to me. You were waiting for that kind of encouragement. You spoke of your heart's sadness and reproached me for saying those hurtful words to you. You said you were annoyed and angry.

It was understandable and acceptable; if I were you, I would probably have been even more angry.

Finally, I admitted to my true feelings. We firmly promised to each other that we would keep in touch and let our relationship continue, we would Skype, email, make phone calls; we would find every possible way to stay together.

The last day before you left, I was working on my day shift. You didn't go out because you wanted to be around me. It was quite hot

The Twin Flame Lover of China and Denmark

in the afternoon; you told me that you needed to take a shower and would be back soon.

You were back with a fresh smell and a fresh look. I noticed your eyes shining, as if there were stars inside your eyes. How charming and wonderful they looked!

But I didn't tell you this was what I had noticed. Instead, I joked with you, saying, "Oskar! Look at your eyes! They are big and round, just like meat balls!"

You didn't mind my sarcasm. Instead, you gently looked at me, asked what kind of interesting things we should do before you leave. You let me decide. I thought for a while, then I told you excitedly that I had never been to a cinema to watch a movie. Just for once, I wanted to be a girl with a lovely boyfriend nearby, holding hands, eating popcorn, drinking Coca Cola!

So we went to the cinema, with excitement in our hearts! By the time we arrived at the cinema, there were no English speaking movies available. So I chose a Chinese comedy movie for us, suggesting you could read the English subtitles.

At the beginning, you were trying to understand the movie by attentively reading the subtitles. However, it must have been difficult or odd for you to understand. Within half an hour, you fell asleep on my shoulder! You were even dribbling like a baby, while there were so many people in the audience frequently laughing out loud.

I couldn't believe what I was seeing. I burst out laughing again!

By the time we came back from the cinema, it was quite late. We found a plot of grass near the hostel. There, we held each other tight and kissed goodbye. I was crying in your arms, not only because I didn't want you to leave, but also because I didn't know when or whether we would ever see each other again. You held me more tightly, lovingly assuring me that you would do everything you could to keep our relationship strong, that you would cherish and support me as much as you could.

Your words made me feel safe. I trusted you totally. Deep down, I even started to think there might be some sort of magical possibility of making our love work.

Next day, which was approximately our 20th day of being together, we went to the airport and said farewell.

We were struggling with our feelings, but we were not sad, because we had promised each other we would keep in touch and we would continue our love. I still wasn't sure when or whether we would ever see each other again, but a certain kind of hope and faith started to grow in my heart.

Chapter 4

Love Torn Asunder, Love Came Back

You had left. I wasn't used to being alone any more. I felt as if a huge part of me had gone with you. My every waking moment was full of our recent memories. I was missing you so much, more than I thought I would.

You called me right after you arrived in India, told me that everything was fine, that you had been missing me very much. I felt happy to hear that. For the next few days, you called me often. However, I noticed that you talked with me less and less and I felt your passion and love was on the wane. I sensed something was wrong.

What was wrong? What had you been thinking during those days? Was it the long distance between us which discouraged you? Did someone tell you this kind of relationship was not going to last long? Did our love feel impossible or unreachable to you? Were you thinking of giving it up?

On the seventh day after you had left, I didn't go to bed after working the night shift but I went to Jin Shan Ling Great Wall with some friends. There, I received a phone call from you. The "Hello" and "How are you?" from you sounded heavy and not very cheerful, which was quite unusual. I immediately knew and feared what you were going to say.

You blurted it out, "I feel that we are really so far away from each other. I can't see you, can't touch you or hug you. I can only speak with you over the phone. For me, it is an incomplete feeling. It feels very difficult and hard. I think, taking the long term into consideration, that we had better break up... it's probably the best solution for both of us..."

Hearing those words, I felt as if I had been struck by thunder. I couldn't believe my most beloved would say such words to me! What made you turn yourself into a playboy? One week earlier, you were promising and loving, reliable and trustful!

I was feeling tired and dizzy, and I did not want to continue our conversation on the phone. So I controlled my pain and replied aggressively, "Okay, breaking up is fine! But now I am very tired, so call me in the evening and let's talk about it then!"

I had a gray day that day, and I suppose you did too.

In the evening, you called on time. In a matter-of-fact kind of voice, you said, "I am still a student, and I will need a lot of time to paint and draw, to prepare for my graduation. I actually have a problem with my heart, which means that I will need to have surgery in the future. I don't really think I will have enough time or energy to take care of our relationship, so we'd better break up now..."

You sounded rational, logical and analytical. As if you were sure you had made the right choice.

It simply shocked me. I wondered how you could erase our earlier words so easily and quickly. I doubted if you were still the same Oskar. I was so disappointed and angry. I was boiling with rage. I wanted to hit out at you!

In a harsh voice, I shouted at you, "Bullshit! All the things you've said are just stupid excuses! Lies! I hate you! Breaking up is fine; let's do it right now! But remember, from now on, never contact me again! Never call me back!"

After saying those words, I hung up immediately, because I didn't want to hear anything else from you or leave you an opportunity to reason with me. I simply wanted to shut the door completely.

I sat on the floor, hugged myself, and started to cry out loud. I even felt quite righteous because deep down I had put all the blame on you by thinking it was totally your fault and wrong, whereas I was the innocent victim one who had got hurt.

For the first time in my life, I tasted what it was like to "break up." Breaking up with you was terrible. It felt bitter, painful and unbearable, as if the very source of my life energy had been suddenly cut off. I couldn't feel any happiness or liveliness any more!

During the following month, I felt lonely and cold. Every day and night, I couldn't help missing you, thinking about you. Somewhere deep down in my heart there was a voice saying, "No, no! This is not true, this is not his truth! He was simply manipulated by his false self to tell those lies to me! He loves me dearly and deeply! He will come back! I want him back! I expect his return!"

Too many feelings and emotions needed to be expressed, I had no way to do so other than to write them down, or rather, to write to you.

Around the beginning of October, I met an English girl named Saffron at the hostel. We liked each other very much and within one or two days, she became one of my wonderful backpacker friends.

One night, Saffron and I went to Hou Hai together. There, we hired a boat and enjoyed the ride on the lake very much. I heard myself laughing so happily! I was full of joy and energy again!

That night, shortly after I arrived at my dormitory, I saw a familiar number calling me. My heart raced! It was my darling YOU!

You finally called me! I had been expecting and waiting for your phone call for an entire month!

Lovingly and sincerely you apologized, spoke your heart, told me that you had been missing me very much every day and night, that you couldn't apply any logic or reason to successfully forget about me. To you, I was too important. Our love was unbreakable.

My frozen heart was immediately melted. I knew you would be back! I knew you still loved me dearly and deeply! My special beloved Oskar had come back!

Together we returned to that blissful heaven again! Everything around us felt so beautiful and wonderful! All was joy. All was love.

The Twin Flame Lover of China and Denmark

Everything was smiling. The whole world was in love, made of love!

You even told me that you had already checked the flights from Copenhagen to Beijing, that you would come back to see me again in the wintertime. You said you would only have 15 days of winter holiday time, and there was no one other than me that you wished to be with.

I felt honored and touched to hear that. I was HAPPY, HAPPY, HAPPY that I would see you again!

Love was flowing between us, growing and flourishing, shining its special light. For the first time, you lovingly said to me, "I love you." You added that even though you had experienced love with other people in the past, you had NEVER felt such strong and intense love before, and that no one had ever made you want to say "I love you." I was the first one, the Special One.

I replied, "Darling! You are also my Special One! I love you, too!"

Chapter 5

Moving to Beijing
Double Happiness Courtyard Hotel

After you left Beijing, I started to feel increasingly dissatisfied with my job. I felt it to be boring and repetitive, shallow and meaningless. I grew tired of just having a good time, having superficial fun. Deep down, I wanted to find something better and deeper to fulfill myself. At that time, the longing was reflected in the thought, "I want to find a similar new job with better pay. I want to become more capable and competent."

I easily found a similar job online and went to the Beijing Double Happiness Courtyard Hotel for an interview. My excellent English speaking skills and relevant working experiences were appreciated by the management and I was asked when I could join the team.

I replied, "Perhaps within two weeks or one month. I haven't quit my current job yet. I really like your hotel and would very much like to work here."

Oliver, the hotel manager, said that they would wait and he hoped it wouldn't take too long.

I then returned to P. Loft and started to ponder when and how I should resign.

Someday in the middle of October, all receptionists at P. Loft were asked to take turns working in the bar for two weeks over the following two months. According to the manager's explanation, in doing so, all staff would become more professional and attentive.

I hated working in bars and didn't want to do it. I was very irritated by their announcement and considered that the manager didn't respect our individual preferences or our personal freedom.

I forced myself to work in the bar for one week; once the week was over, I realized I could not pretend to like it anymore.

One night, I asked the manager if I could go back to working at the reception. He rudely denied my request. We then had an argument and I was asked to leave P. Loft right away.

I remember it clearly; it was on the night of November 14th, 2009. I packed up my small amount of luggage and left P. Loft crying tears of anger. I felt I had been mistreated. They didn't even pay me for the two weeks I had worked in the bar.

Standing alone in the cold wind, the first thing I did was to phone the manager of the Double Happiness Courtyard Hotel. I asked him if I could come the next day and I was told I was more than welcome. They said they would arrange a bed for me in their employees' dormitory.

I felt lucky and relieved to hear that. I had found my next home! In that new home, I would also meet travelers from all over the world and speak English with them. With free food and free accommodation to boot!

After that, I went to the nearby Lama Temple Youth Hostel and checked myself in.

That night, you called. I cried in my loneliness and helplessness, and told you my fears about my uncertain future and my new job.

You listened to me attentively and comforted me with cheerful words. Your words warmed me throughout, and brought me much hope and light. I adored you not only for who you were but also for your loving support. I was deeply grateful for that. I felt incredibly blessed to have a boyfriend like you!

Next day early morning, carried by the magical flow of life, I arrived at the Beijing Double Happiness Courtyard Hotel.

It was a very different place from P. Loft. Their main guests were not young backpackers but older couples and families. I found it to be rather difficult to adapt to this new environment and I suffered much at the beginning, especially because I was such a "free spirit" back then.

However, you helped me out and raised my morale. You gently said to me, "Don't worry, my love, things will become better and better, day by day..."

I remembered this sentence firmly within my heart and every day I started to consciously affirm it to myself. I believed it would become true.

Two weeks later, I became not only qualified to work independently but also the relationship between me and my co-workers was transformed enormously. I started to appreciate my job more and more.

My conscious efforts played a part in achieving this. However, I knew that, without your support, I would never have made it. Therefore, I profoundly thank you, my beloved.

Our love had grown more passionate and sweet. We talked for hours on the phone every day or two and never got tired of it. Our conversations could go on and on, during which we could talk about everything and anything. There was no need to hide anything or hold back. We were simply amazed by the perfect transparency and harmony between us!

So many times, as I was listening to you speaking, I couldn't help thinking to myself, "Listen! How special and familiar his voice sounds! It evokes a very rare sensation in me. I don't know how to express that sensation, but it just feels so UNBELIEVABLE to me. I really feel I have known him for a long, long time."

I was excited to tell you about this feeling and I asked if you felt the same way about my voice.

You replied: "Mm... No, not really, not in the same way as you have described. But I like hearing your voice, especially when you just wake up in the morning. I enjoy calling you at that time; you sound most like the real you..."

When I woke up in the morning, the very first thing I would do was to read the message from you.

"Good morning, Dear Princess, I am so happy that you are mine. I feel I am the luckiest person in the whole world. I will cherish you as much as I can. I wish you a wonderful day. Yours, Oskar."

"Good morning, my lovely sunflower. I just want to tell you I love you so much. Thank you for being mine! I wish you a very nice day today. Your prince, Oskar."

I loved reading your messages; they brought me the sweet sensation of being deeply loved and appreciated. You cannot imagine how energetic and inspired I became after reading them! I felt as if we were on our honeymoon!

One time, at my request, you emailed me a few pictures of yourself at different ages: when you were five, 11, 16 and 20 years old.

I stared at those pictures for a long time, thinking, "To me, Oskar is not that simple. He is more than a lover or a boyfriend. I feel something beyond the ordinary from those pictures... I have definitely met him before! I knew him before we met!"

I put the five-year-old picture of you on my wall and I looked at it every day. One simple glance would make my heart smile with a great sense of satisfaction.

Late December, my birthday was soon approaching. As I wished, you created a drawing for me and mailed it to my hotel.

You wrote, "To the girl I love most in the whole universe. Dear DeDe, Happy Birthday! Before this summer, no one had ever appreciated me like you have. This love feels so beautiful and unbelievable! You are my first real love! I love you for being so engaging, brave, responsible, and diligent. Even though life is hard for you, you always work your way to stay on top. I will not make you cry any more. I will do whatever I can to let us stay together!"

In addition to those words, you created some beautiful drawings as well. You drew me as the most beautiful flower on a patch of green grass, shining with incredible light; you drew our hands holding each other closely; you told me you were smelling my lovely hair.

My heart was deeply touched and I was crying out of joy and bliss. Not only because I loved your letter and the drawings, but deep down, I felt you had touched and understood the deeper side of me. You recognized my wonderful soul qualities and you appreciated them. Your love was beyond the physical or emotional; it was emitted from your very beautiful soul!

STAGE TWO

Ego Emerging

(February 2010-December 2010)

After experiencing a short period of total harmony, the egos begin to emerge and will inevitably lead to an intense emotional crisis, conflicts, pain, and fears that the twins are forced to face. It feels too overwhelming to comprehend and understand, as everything is happening at the deepest soul level. However, hold on, our divine beloved twin is simply helping us by being the divine mirror to reflect our shadow selves, and we, too, become a mirror to their shadow self... Only when the darkness becomes revealed, can we begin to embark upon the path of light and love...

Chapter 6

Happy New Year! I Invited You to My Home Town

You had a 15-days winter holiday during February of 2010. You had already booked your flight and would arrive in Beijing soon. I had been excitedly waiting and counting the days to your arrival, wondering what we could do and where we could go. All I wanted was to create a beautiful and memorable time together.

In the end, I decided to invite you to my home town. I wanted so much to introduce you to my parents and my close relatives; I wanted you to see where I grew up; I wanted you to know more about the real me.

When I was making this decision, I thought, "In my home town, if a girl brings a boy to her home to meet her parents, it is actually indicating that they are most likely going to be married. Should I really invite Oskar to come home with me? If, somehow, we end up not being together, what will those villagers think or say about me? And there have never been any foreigners who came to our small village before. Will they find it unacceptable or abnormal? It is quite risky actually...

"But wait a minute! Why should I care about how other people think or talk about me? I love my Oskar very much and I am sure in this whole world there is nobody other than him whom I would want to bring home! It might sound a bit early now, but I am almost sure that he is the only one I would want to marry!

"For me, this is something very important and meaningful. I want to do it very much! And I will simply do it!"

On the phone, I asked if you would like to come home with me and stay there for a few days. You cheerfully said yes, but I sensed nervousness, as well as excitement. I reassured you by saying, "Don't worry, darling, my parents are very loving and welcoming. I'm sure they will like you a lot!"

After six months' waiting and following my expectations, you were finally coming! We would see each other again!

I was waiting for you at the airport and I kept thinking, "It's been about six months since we have seen each other. Will he have changed? Will he like the way I look now? I bought this new pink sweater and shoes specially for his arrival. I hope he will appreciate that and give me a sweet hug!"

There you were! I saw you! You were lovingly waving your hands to me!

I adored your way of walking. It simply felt charming and special to me. I was enchanted by your unique energy! It was the only type of energy that could make my heart and soul dance with love! I again wondered why the ordinary me deserved having someone as wonderful as you!

We kissed and hugged each other dearly. I felt as if I had returned to a place called home—home of my soul. I wanted so much to tell you, "Darling! Your embrace feels so loving! I love your hugs!"

We stayed in Beijing for a few days, enjoying our time together. After that, we took the 16-hour train ride to my home town.

When we arrived at home, many relatives were already there. I immediately realized they were invited by my parents to welcome us. My father even set up some crackers to celebrate! The house was full of warm greetings and happy faces!

My parents liked you very much and considered you a very reliable and honest person. My grandmother even whispered to me, "Dear, this boy, Oskar, is a very handsome young man!" I felt happy to hear that and I couldn't agree with her more.

The Twin Flame Lover of China and Denmark

My father, who was very good at calligraphy, taught you how to use a brush to write "China" in Chinese. In return, you taught him how to write your name in English. My father's writing was beautifully executed, whereas yours came out not so perfect; it was quite funny. You were confused about where to begin and you ended up writing the word in a completely different way, which made us burst out laughing! We loved it!

During the few days at home, we took lots of nice pictures and had so much fun. I was especially happy that nearly all my family liked you very much, from my nine-year-old cousin to my 89-year-old great grandma.

However, I remember clearly, it was right from this point, that things began to change.

I started to worry and fear greatly about our future. I thought to myself somberly, "I love him so much, to an extent I never knew was possible. This love is so deep and so true, there is no way I can let it go or give it up. I desperately want to be with him!

"But I don't want to be with him in this way forever! Every day we talk on the phone, every six months he comes to Beijing to see me. I feel like a small powerless bird, not capable of doing anything except getting stuck here, counting stars and waiting for his arrival. This doesn't feel right any more! This is becoming more and more dissatisfying and frustrating! I want something more settled and solid! I expect our love to have a concrete result! Not always hanging in the air!

"But what can I do to change all this? I am just an English-speaking receptionist. My family is not rich and, in fact, I need to support them once in a while. I feel powerless and helpless to change anything. I feel our reality is too difficult to change, or rather, it is impossible!

"Besides, my beloved Oskar is so wonderful and charming, whereas I am just so plain." I started to feel that I was probably not good enough for him. "What if one day he says he doesn't love me any more? What am I going to do? Would my whole world crash then? I fear the possibility of losing him; it's something I simply could not bear..."

My previous bright colorful happiness started to turn grey, and so did yours.

After we came back to Beijing, during our daily conversations, you started to talk about famous writers, art, politics and world affairs with me. You asked if I knew certain people, what I thought about this and that. You expected me to follow what you were saying and give some constructive feedback.

How much I wished I was able to do that! But I failed because I was never interested in such things. My replies were often, "No, sorry, I don't know who he is. Sorry, can you explain that? I've never heard of it before..."

While saying those words to you, I felt as if my heart was falling into an icy hole. I felt very sorry for my ignorance. I felt very inferior.

Soon afterwards, red-faced and embarrassed, and in a very bitter voice, I frankly told you that I had actually never read any newspapers or books, that I didn't really know what you were saying.

You couldn't believe it. You felt shocked and disappointed to hear that. You stopped talking and sat silently thinking. You were sitting right next to me but you felt so far away. For the first time, I noticed your eyes had become cold and distant.

I guessed you were probably struggling with thoughts such as, "How could this be possible? How could she not even know these ordinary, everyday things? This is very hard for me to accept, I doubt if..."

As I was trying to read your mind, I was fearfully thinking, "He has now found out about my faults and shortcomings. He is probably concluding that I am not the right one or the perfect one for him. Perhaps he is even seeing me as a very undeveloped person without any depth or knowledge. Will he regret having been with me? Will he still love me?"

The Twin Flame Lover of China and Denmark

Yes, you continued loving me, in spite of your doubts and judgments. And I loved you too, although beset with deep worries and fears.

Fifteen days went by so quickly, and soon you had to leave. For the second time, we went to the airport and said farewell, our hearts in turmoil. I didn't feel too sad because you had already told me that you would come to Beijing again during the summer and would stay with me for two months. I felt happy to hear that, but meanwhile, everything felt ominous.

It was as if from then on, our love was no longer pure or whole any more, as if the bright colors of our rainbow started to fade away. I intuitively sensed and feared that one phase was over, and that the coming one would be hard and difficult.

Chapter 7

We Are Very Confused!

After your return to Denmark, you started calling and messaging me as before. However, I sensed it was not done out of genuine passion or love any more, rather out of obligation, following a routine.

We talked much less than before, and the degree of intimacy was decreasing day by day. I concluded it was something out of my control and I felt sad about it. Meanwhile, my worries and fears intensified.

On the seventh day after your leaving, you called me as usual, said hello and asked how I was. You sounded aggressive. I sensed you were struggling with your hidden anger and confusion.

What exactly were your thoughts?

We really didn't say much on the phone. The short conversation left both of us feeling somehow cold and confused.

After our conversation, I was seized by a deep sense of fear. Fear of losing you!

For the first time in my life, I asked myself seriously, "Who am I? What can I do? Why do I feel so ignorant and useless? My inner world feels so empty and empoverished to me now! Apart from the fact that I am good at speaking English, I can find nothing else special about myself. Obviously a person such as me is not good enough for my Oskar! Is it too late now? What can I do to change myself in order to become a worthy match for him? How can I rescue our love?"

The Twin Flame Lover of China and Denmark

Books! I thought about reading some good books to absorb some knowledge and cultivate my inner self.

I went to the nearby Wang Fu Jing bookstore and started searching. I was sure I wanted to find a simple and interesting English book to read, because I liked English and wanted to improve my language skills.

I was immediately attracted to *The Diary of a Young Girl* by Anne Frank. I read its brief introduction and a few pages inside the book, and decided to buy it. I was thrilled to discover it was a true story based on Anne's diaries; I enjoyed reading about her inner world and feelings.

For the next few months, I continued reading this book. Often her writing reduced me to tears. Her tragic feelings mirrored mine. I found my heart constantly vacillating between joy and anxiety. On the one hand, I was excitedly making all kinds of plans and preparations for our summer holiday; on the other hand, I couldn't control my innermost feelings, as they felt so anxious and unsure!

I worried, "What is awaiting us in the future? Is it going to be a disaster or joy?"

These thoughts preoccupied me, until your arrival became imminent.

This time, your flight would arrive at Guangzhou instead of Beijing. Therefore, I went to Guangzhou three days prior to your arrival.

You called me while I was in Guangzhou and said, "I don't know why and how, but I have been feeling very confused! I have never experienced a love like this before! I..."

I didn't really know what you were referring to. Your words made me feel confused, too! I couldn't think what to say. I fell silent and thought, "What do you mean, you are confused? What do you mean, you've never experienced a love like this before? Every love is supposed to be different! Are you saying there is something wrong or weird about our love?"

The Twin Flame Lover of China and Denmark

It was a short conversation, the last one before your arrival. We hung up, each leaving the other feeling insecure and worried. However, at the same time, we both looked forward to seeing each other the very next day.

Finally after four months, there you were! You hadn't changed much, except you were wearing a pair of flip flops. I asked what had happened to your lovely trainers. You said you had given them to your Indian friend Pascal, because he liked them very much and had never had a pair of shoes like that before.

I admired your kindness and your consideration for others.

Soon, we were sitting on the shuttle, on the way to the hostel where we would stay for a few days. We kept hugging and kissing each other, feelings of intimacy overwhelming us. It felt incredibly intense and deep, as if no other kind of happiness could compare with it. No other person could take the special place that we had for each other in each other's hearts. It was something too beautiful to believe, too rare to understand, too powerful to behold.

All my previous worries and fears suddenly disappeared. I felt relieved and I concluded, "Nothing was wrong, nothing is wrong, everything is going to be all right!"

However, it was too early to assume that. The temporary wonderful joy of seeing each other again soon faded away, replaced by the uncomfortable and unpleasant energy between us.

On the second day, when we were eating barbecue food somewhere on the street, you looked very annoyed and upset, and didn't really speak much with me. I felt I was being rejected and unappreciated. I didn't know what to do about it and I started to find fault with myself.

I thought, "Look, my Oskar looks so good with his T-shirt and shorts on. He is as charming and adorable as ever! But what about me?" I started to feel that the way I dressed didn't match the way he looked. I felt like a poor little girl when standing next to him, whereas I desperately wanted to feel like a shining and beautiful star that is deeply appreciated and loved.

I began to consider changing my outlook to a higher and better mindset. But it was not something I was capable of at the time. My feelings of inferiority continued.

I was upset that you didn't hold my hand when we walked into the hostel; I was grieved that you just couldn't accept the way I was; I questioned why I was no more a Dear Princess in your heart; I wondered why we felt so distant when we were lying right next to each other; I felt miserable about all these things.

We knew something was wrong between us, but we didn't dare to talk about it. We were holding back, hiding our true feelings, struggling and suffering.

As planned, three days later, we took the train from Guangzhou to Guilin. All the way, we hardly spoke, we had no joy to share, no love to feel, as if we had suddenly become two strangers.

It hurt. I simply couldn't bear the cold silence and unloving energy between us. To me, it felt like a living hell. I wanted to end the pain as soon as possible. Back then, the only solution that came to my mind was to break up with you.

I concluded, "I want so much to be close to you, to your heart and soul. I want us to be equal and dear to each other as we were before. This time last year, we were one. Our souls were lovingly speaking to each other! But, look at us now! Why? Why has everything changed so much?

"Is it because I am not good enough for you? Perhaps...

"You come from a developed country–Denmark. I have heard that your country's welfare system is one of the best in the world. Besides, your parents are top doctors in Denmark and you probably don't have family responsibilities as I do. Our culture and family backgrounds are very different!

"You know what you want to do with your life in the future; you want to become a great artist! But for me everything is uncertain. I have no well-thought out career plan. Such a person like me is definitely not qualified to deserve someone like you. I shouldn't stand in your way.

"Your love for me is no longer as strong and deep as it was. I feel you are going to leave me anyway, since our mindsets, likes and interests are so different. In other words, we are obviously not compatible! You didn't suggest breaking up because you didn't want to hurt me. But I should set you free, because I am aware of it already. I'd better do it... For you, this would probably be the best result."

We arrived at Guilin next day at noon and checked into a youth hostel. There were no double rooms available, so we took the six-bed dormitory instead, sharing it with a few other travelers.

Late in the afternoon, we walked to a forest nearby. There, I proposed breaking up, adding that we should cherish the last days of being together.

You were rather shocked to hear that. You thought for a while, and then, you hesitantly replied, "Mm... Thank you for your consideration for my welfare. I believe that you, too, will find your love and live a happy and fulfilling life. I agree with your 'countdown' proposal; it is probably the best for both of us."

The break up agreement relieved our minds to a certain extent, but it left our hearts struggling, "Is this really the right solution? Do I really want to do this?"

We then started to walk back, holding hands tightly.

That night, around 2 or 3 a.m., I suddenly woke up, and heard you calling my name. Your voice sounded very weak and I immediately sensed something was wrong.

You muttered: "DeDe, I am ill. I feel so cold... I am trembling..."

Tremulously I touched your forehead. It was bathed in cold sweat. But it was summertime, so how could that be?

I didn't really know what to do but I felt instinctively that if we embraced each other, I would warm you and make you feel better.

As I was holding you tightly, I felt as if I was hugging love or life, even though I didn't really know what they were. A magical sensation

The Twin Flame Lover of China and Denmark

was flowing all around me.

You fell asleep shortly. You were breathing peacefully and were not sweating any more. I felt relieved.

I was wide awake and I was speaking to you in my mind, "Darling Oskar, even if it takes my life, I will save you at any cost! Because you are so important and special to me! I never wanted you to walk away from me. Please forgive me for the words I said. I love you!"

Early next morning, you had recovered and we continued our journey.

Originally, we had planned to take trains and buses all the way to my home town. We thought it would be fun to travel that way. However, we soon realized that it was tiring and uninteresting. You then suggested buying a motorbike to continue our trip.

You told me that you had seen many people riding motorbikes when you were traveling in India and you had admired that mode of travel very much. A very nice Indian boy had even taught you how to ride. Since then, you had always dreamed of traveling by motorbike. Now you would make your "motorbike dream" come true.

I was startled but I admired your courage. It was several thousand miles from where we were to my home town in Hubei. We had to pass through many big and small towns we did not know. It was a challenge! But meanwhile, it felt exotic and interesting!

We suffered from the heat but washed off the dust in the rain. We ate simply and lived cheaply. We felt so cool riding through the starry nights. We kissed passionately to celebrate the beauty and the freedom we were experiencing. We had much joy and fun.

I complimented you, "Oskar! With your helmet on, you look like the most handsome construction worker in the whole world! You are charming!"

A few days later, on a cold rainy day, you laughingly said to me, "Darling, I think you really look lovely with your raincoat on! In fact, I would say this is your most beautiful look yet!"

However, along with the love we shared, there were moments of sadness and heaviness. After all, we were "counting down" our days.

Fifteen days later, we finally arrived at my parents' house.

My parents were delighted to see you again, together with my grandparents and uncles. They were amused by the fact that both of us were wearing flip flops and wondered how we had made it. They admired our courage and determination.

You helped with the harvesting. My parents appreciated that very much and complimented you a lot. You took many lovely pictures for them, which they cherish still.

My father sighed and said to me that it would be better if we were just friends, because it was unrealistic for us to have a serious relationship. My mother still felt it hard to believe that her daughter's boyfriend was from Denmark and that he had been having meals with us using chopsticks. My sister felt quite upset because she could hardly speak any English and so struggled to communicate with you.

Me? Like you, I was lost in confusion.

Chapter 8

Goodbye Forever???

Thanks to my manager Luo Rong, who generously lent one of her apartments to us for free, we had a lovely house in Beijing to stay in for the next month, or rather, the last month?

It was the first time that my manager had met you. She couldn't speak any English but she sensed your equanimity and good energy. She whispered to me, "DeDe, your boyfriend Oskar is quite a handsome young man! I hope you two will enjoy your stay here."

We thanked her for her kindness and she then left with a warm smile on her face.

That month, I had to work at my hotel. This meant my time and energy were divided between my job and you. I experienced joy as well as chaos.

I used to feel happy and excited about my job and I enjoyed so much interacting with our guests. However, as I was projecting my frustration from our relationship onto almost every area of my life, I started to feel fed up with my work. Most of the time when I was working I felt rather tired and unfulfilled.

Most of the time you would stay at home, surfing the Net, reading and painting. Sometimes you would come to my hotel to teach my manager's daughter painting; at other times we would go out somewhere. We enjoyed the luxury of being able to see and hug each other every day, but at the same time we felt anxious and insecure about our "rootless" love. Meanwhile, conflicts had arisen, and we started to argue.

The Twin Flame Lover of China and Denmark

Oskar: "Why are you home so late? You said you would be back within two hours. It's been four hours..."

DeDe: "Why are you so angry and so upset? I just happened to meet my friend Lily and we talked for a while. Do you have to be such a 'clock watcher'?"

Oskar: "At least you should phone me or text me so that I know what is going on. I don't like being left here alone... You should keep your word..."

I realized that I was in the wrong. I apologized and eased your bad mood with a hug and a kiss.

A few days later, after we walked out of the supermarket:

DeDe: "Hey, honey, can you take this bag please? It's a little bit heavy for me. Besides, I don't like the fact that I am the one who carries the bags when I am walking with you."

Oskar: "Why do you have so many 'should' or 'should not' on your mind? I really don't like it when you say a boy should do something and a girl should do something else. In my country, men and women are equal. We don't have such unreasonable rules like this!"

DeDe: "But in my country it's different! Men are supposed to act like gentlemen!"

Reluctantly, you took the bag. I acted as if I was the winner, but deep down, I felt like a loser.

In addition we argued about the right way to hang our clothes, who should wash the dishes after a meal, why you had so many bad movies stored on your computer, why I didn't know anything about some famous building, etc.

Our personality traits were put under the spotlight and we felt upset and annoyed on those occasions. You felt aggressive and belligerent towards me, whereas I looked passive and defensive to you.

However, when we were able to fully embrace each other's energy or we could just live in the now, love began to flow again.

You covered your face with your hands, preparing a surprise.

The Twin Flame Lover of China and Denmark

Then a few seconds later you revealed a funny face; and then came another interesting look. Your lovely innocence and expressiveness were just like a little five-year-old boy's. I was very amused and I felt my heart fill with joy.

DeDe: "Darling Oskar! You are very funny! I want to know if you are equally childlike when you are with your parents or friends in Denmark!"

Oskar: "No no, not really. In fact, when I am with my parents, I always seem to be quite serious. Sometimes my Mom wants to kiss me when I am back home, and I avoid such intimacy most of the times. I feel very good and comfortable when I am with my best friend Simon, but I have never acted like this before."

DeDe: "So, are you saying I am the only one who can bring out your childlike self? And you feel totally at ease with that and even happy about it?"

Oskar: "Yes..."

I felt privileged and honored to hear that.

DeDe: "Honey, what did you look like when you were at school? Were you popular? Were you the most handsome boy in class?"

Oskar: "No no... I was never the most handsome boy. My classmates always thought me rather weird and sometimes I got "special attention" because of it. In fact, I like being weird! I remember when I and two of my classmates formed our own 'Community of Weird People.' But it only lasted for a few days..."

DeDe: "You were also weird? Me too! I always feel I am different than other people around me! I have a strange feeling that I actually come from another world. Sometimes I look at the stars and I feel I have an intimate connection with them!"

Oskar: "Okay... well... but that probably sounds too weird..."

DeDe: "Okay. Let's not talk about it then. Now, I want you to be a gorilla! The lovely gorilla you were last time!"

For my enjoyment, you transformed yourself into a gorilla. You started walking and even making noises like they do, touching and caressing me, full of lovingness and tenderness. I felt bathed in love!

Later that night, you even offered me a foot massage. You gently put my feet into a basin full of warm water, and then you washed them carefully. I felt I was spoiled by love!

At those moments, I thought to myself, "This is the real you, my real Oskar. He loves me deeply, deeply... even more than he or I realize. But we may have great difficulty acknowledging and handling it."

One day, we went to Hou Hai Lake, there we kissed and talked.

DeDe: "Look! So many lovely willow trees over there! The beautiful lake, the blue sky, the fishermen, what a lovely day! Do you like this place?"

Oskar: "Yes, very much. I am enjoying all of this."

DeDe: "But you look a little sad. Are you thinking about us?"

Oskar: "Yes."

DeDe: "Haven't we agreed that we will stop seeing each other? Both of us are already aware that we are not that compatible, right? At least I have admitted that, more specifically, you deserve someone better..."

You didn't say anything, lost in thought. A few seconds later, I felt as if you suddenly "woke up" and realized something important. With great certainty and excitement, you said to me, "I have finally realized what I love about you! I love your Spirit!"

Confused, I thought, "He says he loves my spirit? But do I have one? Does he mean he appreciates my modest spirit by the fact that I admitted I am not good enough for him or does he love something within me which is higher than me...?"

I didn't answer you. We continued our walk.

A few minutes later, an old Chinese lady approached us and looked at us from head to toe. It felt very strange to both of us. In the end, the lady said to me, "Girl! You are lucky! I can tell your boyfriend is a very good-hearted young man, unlike the other western boys I've seen. Good luck to your love!"

The Twin Flame Lover of China and Denmark

I felt happy to hear those words from a stranger, but at the same time I doubted the luck part.

I didn't translate those words for you; instead, I simply told you she thought you were a lovely young man. You smiled sweetly.

Time flew so quickly, through our joy and sorrow, blended with our uncertainty and yet the undeniable commitment of the heart.

It was time to face separation again, or rather, goodbye forever?

Sitting on the sofa, thinking about the following day, you suddenly started to cry. Tears streamed down your cheeks; you let them fall. You were finally not a strong man any more, but a vulnerable little boy who was crying from the soul.

Darling, it was the first time I had seen you cry. I felt your unspeakable pain and confusion; they resonated with my own sorrow and struggle. I couldn't find any words to comfort you, so I hugged you, and we cried in each other's arms.

The next day, for the third time, we went to the airport. On the way, I didn't say much, I simply felt as if every piece of me was falling apart. In tears, I thought, "What does this mean? Does it mean I will never, ever see my beloved Oskar again? I will never be able to hug or kiss him again? No, this cannot be happening to me! I don't agree with it! I don't want this!"

Only half an hour later, you had to go. I started to cry in your arms. I felt my every single cell and bones were being torn apart by an unbearable pain, the pain of separation, the pain of the soul. I felt as if a part of me was being cut off!

I felt I must have been cursed and that God must have made a serious mistake. Why did She/He treat us with such cruelty? Why let us fall in love so deeply but continue to separate us? This was unfair!! Why all this pain and suffering? Why? Why?

In all my anger and confusion, I began to hate Destiny.

Time was up, you had to go. I stopped crying and I no longer knew what to do. I felt paralyzed. You gently kissed my forehead and said to me, "My love, you are wonderful."

The Twin Flame Lover of China and Denmark

You were waving goodbye to me as you were walking through the gate. I didn't say or do anything in return, because I had already crashed. My only question was, "How will I survive?"

Chapter 9

The Crisis Continues

I arrived at my dormitory, totally exhausted and broken-hearted. It was about 7 o'clock in the morning, my co-workers were still sleeping. I threw myself onto my bed and started to cry. I tried to be quiet so that they wouldn't be woken up. But the pain was too intense to control. Not wanting to disturb them, I went outside to find a private place to give way to my emotion.

In a small corner located on the roof of our hotel, I cried desperately for half an hour, feeling the whole world was falling in on me. Amidst all the pain and sorrow, a decision was made, "From today on, I will start writing a diary! I must exorcise my emotions and feelings. No one around me can really understand what I am feeling. Therefore, I must learn how to talk to myself!"

For the next few days, I had no desire to talk, eat or sleep. I was merely a body with a dead soul. I felt numb, as if I couldn't find any reason to continue living. Every day after work, I was tormented with thoughts such as, "Does Oskar love me or not? If he does, why did he leave me alone like this? Why did he so easily give up on our love? Does this mean that he does not love me?

"But no, I felt his love! My heart felt it! He loves me deeply!

"But why did he sometimes distance himself from me? Why the coldness and judgment? Why did we experience so many painful emotions? Why did I lose myself? Why did I do and say some things that were not from my heart? Why did everything become so heavy and dark?

The Twin Flame Lover of China and Denmark

"I really don't understand what was going on between us! When we were in harmony, everything was fine and beautiful, all was well. It was like heavenly joy! But when we were not, everything became a huge disaster. The pain and the struggle we felt were extremely intense. It is definitely something too overwhelming to comprehend. This is not common behavior! Ours is a unique kind of love!"

I wrote down many words similar to these in my diary. And while I was writing, one meter away from me there were my co-workers enjoying television and snacks. A few months ago, I was like them. But now, I was no longer the same person. My body felt so heavy and so painful, and so did my mind and soul. I asked myself in despair, "When will I be happy again?"

A few days after your departure, I had a mysterious dream. Sometime around dawn, I dreamed that the wind was blowing, not very strongly, but strongly enough to wake up all the unknown plants and the grasses, which had somehow become alive and aware. The plants, the air, the energy in the air, as well as other invisible beings all around, all possessed very heightened and sensitive 'knowingness.' They were waiting for something, or rather, they knew something was going to happen.

Above them was the indigo mystical sky, deeper than ever. All of a sudden, a star appeared somewhere in the sky. Immediately a very powerful light struck and 'awakened' the star, which then shone with extra brilliance. But then, in a blink of an eye, everything disappeared.

I woke up from the dream. I could remember everything so clearly, as if it were real. It was hard to describe my strange feelings but I felt as if my very soul had been shocked and shaken. It was about six o'clock in the morning. I wrote down this dream in my diary.

Much later I understood the symbolic meaning of this dream. The star was my spirit, facing the unbearable loss of Oskar. Then I started to wake up. This marked the very beginning of my spiritual awakening.

Two or three days later, you called me, saying that you could not let our love go and that you wanted to continue our relationship.

This was something I had strongly foreseen. I just knew you would call me. I knew you wouldn't leave me like that. As I had always felt before, "Oskar loves me very much, more than he realizes."

You were waiting for my reply on the phone. My heart wanted to say no because I knew we were not ready, since the very root of our problems was not resolved and our wounds were not healed. Everything was still in confusion and our hearts were still in turmoil. If we came together in this way, the consequences could become even worse!

But the mind said yes, because I would rather love with a painful heart than not love at all. But I never wanted to experience the unbearable pain of losing you again.

So we were once more together. But from that moment on fear started to take hold of me, controlling my every word and action. It led me to never say or do anything to offend you, so that you wouldn't feel angry and walk away. The terrible fear of losing you sometimes even made me tremble.

I didn't know what you were thinking or how exactly you were feeling, but I clearly sensed your anger and frustration. You felt upset about the way I was acting and you didn't like the new false and fearful me. You probably knew why I had changed and you felt rather guilty about it.

On one occasion, during a phone conversation, I gave in to you again, acting more passively than ever. You finally couldn't hide your feelings any more and spoke to me rather provocatively. That immediately triggered my anger and I decided to fight back.

DeDe: "Please mind your words! Don't talk to me like that!"

You apologized sincerely, saying, "I'm sorry. Sometimes I wish you could act in a more assertive way..."

That was all you said. But it was obviously not all you wanted to say. I assumed you probably wanted to continue, saying something like, "I really want to experience the real you, the real DeDe who can stand up for herself courageously, for dignity, for love, and for freedom."

But unfortunately, back then, all my courage was asleep. Fear dominated me.

Day by day, night by night, it became very painful to continue our love. We clearly felt that our love was in danger and in a serious crisis.

One day, you told me one of your teachers highly encouraged you to go to Berlin and join an excellent study group, founded by a very famous German artist. You would even have many opportunities to meet the artist in person and improve your painting skills. You asked me if you should go.

My first thought was, "You are going to study in Berlin and become an apprentice to a very famous German artist. You will learn something more about art and painting. That sounds very impressive. Your future is bright.

"What about me? What am I doing here? I am simply a receptionist. My future is quite gray. There is a huge gulf between us. What if you happen to meet a beautiful girl who shares your interests and likes during your stay there? What if you find her fascinating? Very dangerous! You should not go there!"

Of course I didn't share those pitiful thoughts with you. Instead, I passionately encouraged you by saying, "Of course you should go! Such a great opportunity! It will be very good for your future. Maybe you will learn some creative painting skills while you are there. Go!"

Two weeks later, you arrived in Berlin.

Things didn't go as I had feared, or as you had expected. Instead, you encountered obstacles and difficulties. You told me that most of the students there talked with each other in German instead of English, so you had difficulty communicating with them. Moreover, every time you tried to make an appointment with the famous artist, he always seemed too busy.

When you told me these things, you sounded rather low and disappointed. I could understand. I, too, felt quite sorry about your situation. I wanted so much to raise your spirits, but I just didn't know what to say. I felt I was being useless.

Another night, over the phone, I asked if the situation had improved. You said no, it was still the same. I sensed you sounded even lower. But still, I could not find any positive words to comfort you.

We hung up soon after that, both feeling cold inside.

I couldn't fall asleep and I kept worrying about your situation. I felt so useless and so stupid that I was not able to help you out.

In order to make you feel a little bit better, or rather, in order to ease my bad feelings, I sent you a cheer-up message, telling you not to worry and that things would improve.

You didn't reply. I concluded that I was unappreciated and my words didn't really count. As a result, I felt much worse and even more stupid.

Sadly, I thought, "My Oskar is in a very difficult situation. He needs love and support. But we are both feeling disappointed to find out that I, as his beloved one, have failed to offer him any hope or faith. What a failure! What an embarrassing feeling!"

Why had our love come to this? The truth is that since we had met each other, Oskar was always the supporter, whereas I was always the weaker one. I kept telling him all my problems and worries, as if he was my emotional crutch. I received so much love and support from him, but I never really knew how to give or share in return.

I felt ashamed to admit these truths and I felt our love had failed to pass the test. Moreover, I sensed and feared something else was probably on its way.

STAGE THREE

Temporary Return (December 2010-August 2011)

The Twin Flame love is beyond physical and emotional. It asks for unconditional love and total acceptance, which is unlike any other relationship the twins had experienced or heard of before. The battle between the ego and the heart is fierce and difficult and thus it can make the twins feel intensely confused and lost. At this stage, the light of their divine love shines upon them and brings them back together for the purpose of fostering further development and improvement of their mind and consciousness, as well as pre-organizing the flow of energy between them that is soon to follow...

Chapter 10

The Book and the Return

You hadn't contacted me for a few days. I intuitively knew what you were thinking. My heart was suffering in limbo and I decided to find a solution.

I was working alone at reception on the night shift. After I had finished my work, I dialed your phone number. After only a few minutes of conversation, came the suggestion, "Let's break up."

I hung up the phone and started to cry, sobbing in desperation. But strangely, the intense sadness did not overwhelm my heart. Instead, I started to think calmly, "Why? Why all this unbearable pain and confusion? There must be a reason. But who can tell me what it is? Who can help me?"

Suddenly, I noticed that soon, at 4 a.m., a special guest would check out. I remembered that when she had walked into our hotel I immediately had sensed at that time that she was somehow different than most guests I had ever met. To me, it seemed as if she possessed some high awareness and was already on a spiritual path.

My mind was led to think, "In China, the number four is seen to be a very unlucky number because the way it is pronounced is very similar to the word death. However, for me, it has always been a very lucky number. I have just broken up with my beloved Oskar and I desperately want to find an answer to everything. And this special guest is checking out this morning at 4 a.m....Could it be that she perhaps holds the key? This is an opportunity, and I should take it! If I learn nothing, I have lost nothing. But if I find something out, I

The Twin Flame Lover of China and Denmark

win!"

The special guest arrived on time. After carrying out the checking out procedure, I gathered all my courage and decided to ask my questions.

DeDe: "M'am, excuse me, could you perhaps spare me a minute? I know this might sound very crazy or strange, but I really need your help and I feel you might be able to help me.

"One hour ago I broke up with my boyfriend whom I love very much. The relationship between us has been extremely painful and confusing. I have totally lost myself. I really want to find out why and I truly need some profound answers..."

"Have you ever been in a similar situation before? Have you read any books which have helped you?"

She was listening to me attentively. I could sense her care was real and sincere. She said to me, "Thank you very much for trusting me. Actually, I was in a similar situation to yours many years ago. I had the same problem with my current husband. We were in a serious crisis and we didn't see or contact each other for a whole year. But now, we are happily married.

"I know there is a book that will definitely help you and answer some of your questions. The book is called *Living Through the Meantime*. It will help you find yourself and the love you want. It's a wonderful book written by Iyanla Vanzant. She is a very well known spiritual counselor in my country. Once I even met her in person when I needed help the most. I received so much wise advice from her. I sincerely hope this book will help you, too."

I was so grateful for her help. I felt as if I had suddenly found hope and light!

Next day, I ordered the book online. Three days later, it arrived.

After reading the preface and the first few pages, I excitedly thought, "This is the divine book I was longing for! This is the book I desperately needed. This must be magic! That lady must be the angel sent by God to help me out! I am so happy that I asked my question!"

For the next three months, I continued reading this book, meanwhile thinking about you, writing my thoughts, and reflecting on our past. Day by day, night by night, I felt as if the wise words and the healing energy of this book were cleansing my mind and soul. My wounds were cured and my mind was not toxic any more; everything felt clean and pure.

Hugely relieved I concluded, "It's all up to me. I am the one who must take total responsibility for my well-being and happiness. My beloved Oskar is my Divine Mirror. He reflected my ego, my lack of self confidence and self love. I need not blame him or feel anger toward him anymore. Instead, I will be grateful for all the heavenly love and joy he has brought into my life.

I now fully understood that in order to live a truly happy and fulfilling life I have to know who I really am and what my life work is. It is about knowing the self in a deeper way and about achieving self-realization.

"I need to find those important answers about myself, about life, about my mission and vision. I have a long way to go. I am not yet ready!"

With love and gratitude, I finally could accept your leaving with a peaceful heart. I no longer felt the pain and the struggle; all my inclinations to hate, to control and to obsess had vanished.

Sincerely, I was speaking to you in my mind, "Darling Oskar, you are the divine loving angel sent by God to help me realize all these things. Thank you for all your sweet love and inspiration. I now set you free and I bless you with my heart and soul. I wish you well, my love."

That same night, my spirit was uplifted and I felt incredibly happy. My roommates and I even sang happily in our dormitory for two hours. All of us were immersed in tremendous joy and excitement. We were celebrating life, talking about love and dreaming of our future.

The Twin Flame Lover of China and Denmark

I went to bed quite late that night. In that mysterious dreamland, I saw a very big and shining full moon.

In China, the full moon often symbolizes reunion. It usually means that some of our old friends, relatives, or lovers will probably visit us soon.

However, I expected nothing and that morning I went straight to work. Strangely, that whole morning I felt very happy and I even started to appreciate everything with love. I was in an indescribably blissful state.

At that most wonderful moment, I heard my phone receive a message and I wondered who it was from.

It was you—my Darling Oskar! My heart turned somersaults!

Your words were full of love and gentleness; you wrote that three days ago you had sent me an important email and that you had anxiously been waiting for my reply. You had finally sent me a message, which I had been awaiting for for three whole months! I had been checking my email almost every day just to see if you would write. But I had been feeling so wonderful recently that I hadn't checked my email for one whole week!

My joy and excitement were beyond words; I quickly opened my email.

You confessed you had been loving and missing me very much, that you had been struggling with your feelings and thoughts a lot. In the end, you realized you could not let go of me or give up our love. You were coming back! You asked me if you would still be welcomed or not.

Yes! Of course! Darling! You were more than welcome to come back! I had been desperately waiting for that!

It was some time around December, winter had already arrived. However, for us, it was lovely summer. Because our love had magically transformed the season. You were coming back! In one month, you would fly to Beijing to see me again! I couldn't believe this was really happening!

We talked for about three hours on the phone that night. The previous judgment, distance, coldness were all banished by the powerful light of our love. Our hearts and minds had become one. We were back in our original heaven!

It had been a very difficult test, but we had made it. Love had conquered the ego.

For the following week, my mood was summer-like. Every day, all I felt were pure joy and excitement; I felt I couldn't be happier.

However, when thinking about reality and our future, I became frustrated again.

I worried, "I still don't know what I want to do with my life in the future. I am aware that I will need much time and energy to find and fulfill my purpose. Besides, the same old problem 'how can we really be together?' has not been resolved."

I felt so happy that you were coming back. But after all this time, were we going to walk the same old path again? I, waiting for you under the moon, and you coming to Beijing to visit me twice a year?

No! That path had been unsatisfying and painful to us, it was a dead path that would never lead us anywhere! We needed a new path! One that could take us toward a rainbow and move us closer to hope. We needed a miracle!

Soon, you were coming; what should I do?

Perhaps I should have set you free. Not because I thought I was not good enough for you any more, but because I needed to find and follow my own path. In other words, the timing was not right; it felt like our love should be frozen for a period of time before we become truly ready...

"Yes, this was the right thing to do. A few days after your arrival, I will find a good time to talk to you about it."

I wrote you a very long email, in which I implied that I would perhaps need a long time to search for my path and fulfill my life.

Your letter was hand-written. You had scanned the paper and emailed it to me.

The Twin Flame Lover of China and Denmark

You wrote, "Dear DeDe, during our summertime together, I realized that sometimes I was easily carried away by my own desires and needs; as a result of this, I must have hurt your feelings a lot. I am SORRY! Please forgive me!

"If you are going to look for your dream or path, I will never stand in your way. I will only respect and support your choice and do as much as I can to help you.

"In 2009, after I left you in Beijing, I was surprised to find out that you seemed to have so many problems and troubles; we soon began to establish our roles as the Supporter (I) and the Dependent (You).

"That relationship role left me with a very unpleasant feeling for a long time. I felt that I wasn't getting the kind of progress or inputs that I expected and wanted from our relationship.

"But that won't stop me from loving you or continuing our relationship. Instead, after hearing this, I hope you will still tell me your troubles or problems. Please don't hide them; I would like to listen to them and help you!

"Our love is rather difficult; we have to prepare for a 'long fight' for its future victory, and that is not going to be easy. But we should just listen to our hearts. My heart says, I want to stay with you!"

Your honesty and sincerity touched my very heart and soul. I cried out for joy.

You told me that you had prepared some gifts for me, asking me whether there was anything in particular I would like to have.

I replied, "No, not really, you are the most precious gift! Mm... but wait a minute! I would like to have a very special heart-shaped necklace! It should not be an expensive one but definitely a very unique one. And maybe, I would also like to have a small package of Danish candy. We've known each other for a long time but I have never tasted any candies from your country..."

You laughed a little over my "candy request," but gently said that you would bring some for me.

The Twin Flame Lover of China and Denmark

I wanted to know what kind of presents you had prepared. You laughingly said, "Mm... It's a secret!"

Chapter 11

The Six Presents, the Fourth Separation

*I*t was your fourth visit to Beijing. I thanked whatever gods had brought us back together. I concluded we must be the special, blessed ones.

My manager Luo Rong lent her apartment to us for free for the second time; my co-worker Yan helped clean the house and my sister pumped up many colorful balloons for us, which I stuck on the wall to decorate our house, or rather, to welcome your return.

When we arrived at the house, you saw all the preparation work I had done and you felt happy and touched. You lovingly said to me, "Thank you, my love."

That night we talked, hugged and bonded intimately in a place called Heaven.

Early next morning, I excitedly opened the gifts you had prepared for me. There were six in total. All had been carefully wrapped in typical lovely Danish paper. Tears of joy immediately streamed from my eyes; I felt I was deeply, wholeheartedly loved by love–by you!

You had printed out a beautiful picture of the Cuan Di Xia village which we had visited in 2009 and you had put the picture into a rainbow colored photo frame–that was my first present.

You told me that you had actually hand painted the frame because you wanted it to be more personal and colorful. You added that you felt Cuan Di Xia was a special and meaningful place to us and that you would never forget the mysterious beauty we experienced that night.

The Twin Flame Lover of China and Denmark

You created a lovely drawing with my name on it and asked someone to print the picture on a new white T-shirt—my second present.

You had gift wrapped your own camera for me, because I didn't have one. You wanted me to travel more and experience the wonderful brilliance of the world—my third present.

You had bought me a heart-shaped necklace with a colorful rainbow image carved inside—my fourth present.

You had painted an interesting drawing on a round wooden frame—my fifth present.

A pack of Danish candy was my sixth present.

You wrote on the gift card, "My dearest DeDe, I have never prepared gifts for anyone with such a joyful and excited heart like this before. I hope you will like them, my love."

Darling! I adored them all! You made me feel as if I were a shining star!

We stayed in Beijing for only three days. We invited all our friends to our place and ate a hot pot together. Much love and joy were shared; everyone could feel that our relationship was as it had been before, that we were simply melting in pure love and total harmony.

However, somewhere in the corner of my mind, a voice was intruding, "When should I tell him about the idea of freezing our love? Or rather, when should I mention breaking up to him? How will he react? Maybe I should wait until we arrive at my parents' house?"

Next day, as planned, we took the train to my home town.

As usual, we were welcomed and loved, just like the sunshine. My parents felt quite happy that we were together again, but meanwhile, like me, their hearts were worrying.

The following evening, when there were only two of us sitting in the room, I proposed breaking up with you. I simply told you that it was impossible for us to have a future, and therefore it would be better to finish this love right now. I also suggested that you should

The Twin Flame Lover of China and Denmark

not ask too many questions and that you should respect my decision, which I had thoroughly thought through.

This was something you had never expected. You could not figure out why and how I was saying this; you were deeply shocked and saddened. You didn't know what to do about it, except allowing yourself to cry quietly.

Your heart was breaking, and mine was also suffering.

You agreed with my proposal, saying that we should cherish the remaining seven days of being together.

How to spend these last seven days? In the end, we decided to go to Shanghai—a place we had never visited. We wanted to experience something new together.

Our Shanghai trip was memorable and beautiful. We concluded we must have found the most delicious beef noodles in the world, that we were so lucky to have dinner in that super lovely restaurant. We chased each other happily on the street, just like two five-year-old children; we visited a renowned park and the museum; we bargained in the clothing market and bought a lovely outfit for your nephew. You laughingly said that you looked forward to seeing how it would look on a small Danish child; I reproached you for not buying the two small unique wooden duck toys in the market. You lovingly eased my bad mood with a big sweet hug.

We were the happy energetic travelers; we were the young lovers who were experiencing the world with great passion and excitement. So many times, I couldn't help feeling that we were just like a married couple!

One night, as we were lying in bed, we started to talk about everything that came into our minds. All of a sudden, confused, you complained, "You know, I have thought about this many times, like where can we settle down and what we should do in the future. If we get married and have kids, where can they go to school? Is it going to be in China or in Denmark? These are very difficult practical problems between us. Sometimes they really make me feel very confused...!"

No, I couldn't believe my ears. I couldn't believe that you had in fact thought about our future, marriage and even children! It meant to me that you deeply, deeply cared!

I hid my shock, and simply asked you, "You really thought about these things before? Why didn't you tell me about it?"

You were puzzled and said to me, "Didn't I tell you all this before?!"

DeDe: "No! You never told me! Just like you never told me I am beautiful..."

Oskar: "Okay... Honey, I am sorry. I really think you are beautiful! Please forgive me if I have truly never said that to you. But maybe... I just didn't say it enough times, right? But you should know you are beautiful, because you are."

Your answer made me laugh. I stopped teasing you and we went on chattering happily.

Time seemed to fly more quickly than ever, especially when we were happy. For the fourth time, we had to separate again, at the same place—Beijing International Airport.

We kissed lovingly and said farewell gently, pretending our hearts were at peace, forcing ourselves to think it was probably the best ending possible.

However, destiny whispered that it was just yet another new beginning.

Chapter 12

"The Alchemist" and the Au Pair Dream

The very first day after your departure, I woke up naturally around 7 o'clock in the morning, remembering clearly the strange dream I'd had.

In my dream, I saw a path. I was inspired by some unknown forces to walk toward it. And the path was the one less travelled.

Messages were transmitted to my consciousness in a strange way that I had never experienced before. I felt awed. In order to clear my mind, I decided to go out for a walk.

While I was walking, a mysterious feeling overwhelmed me, "Today, I feel I was reborn by something or someone. I am going to explore the world with a totally new identity and I am starting to walk toward my own path..."

This was an initiation and an introduction to my spiritual path. I understood this only much later.

Back then, these strange feelings and images didn't hold my attention for long. Within two or three days, I found myself totally lost in thinking about you. I doubted whether I had made the right choice and I deeply wished you could come back.

Love was always there; it had never gone away. Two days later, I received a loving email from you, in which you wrote, "Dearest DeDe, you are special to me. I've never experienced such unbelievable intimacy with anyone before. I love you! I want to be with you!"

Those were the exact same words I wanted to say to you. So I lovingly replied, "Yes." We felt quite happy that we were together again.

However, the sweet joy only lasted about two weeks, because I became extremely frustrated again.

I struggled. "I fear this love! I don't know why, but I am deeply afraid of it! Something within me cannot be at peace with it! Besides, what are we going to do in the future? We are still walking the same old path! Our love is not going to work out...!"

The same old pattern appeared again; again, I decided to end it.

I sent you a rather cold email suggesting that we should break up. At the end, I added, "Please do not write to me again. Thank you."

I could not imagine how hurtful those words felt to you. I never tried to think, how saddened and devastated I would feel if I were you. My mind was totally manipulated by my fear. All I wanted to do was to run away from you. As I had deluded myself previously, I again felt that as long as I could abandon you, I would no longer have to deal with the unbearable pain or the intense struggles any more.

You replied nothing. I felt relieved but heart-broken.

It looked as if I had completely given up on our love, but no! I could never really watch it be defeated by what appeared to be impossible.

Strangely, I found myself starting to think, "I might want to go to Denmark to see what life is like in that country. It does not mean we will settle down there or anything, but I am feeling a strong desire to go there. Maybe I can discover some sort of magical opportunity for us?

"But how can I go there? For a start, it is extremely difficult and expensive to apply for a tourist visa to go to Denmark. Besides, it is not my intention to go there merely as a tourist and stay only for about one month. I want something different! Something that will serve my soul's purpose perfectly! But what can it be? Does it exist? Is it possible?"

My rational mind immediately concluded it was impossible and too risky, but yet my heart couldn't help secretly fantasizing about it.

The Twin Flame Lover of China and Denmark

One night, as usual, I started to write in my diary.

"Dear God: what is your plan? What do you want me to do? Why did you throw me this impossible love? I'd rather die if I cannot be with my Oskar! It is unfair! It is cruel! It is..."

My mind was in overdrive while I was writing, I felt as if my head was going to explode, because it seemed like such an extreme struggle. At that very moment, something magical happened.

I asked myself a very strange question, "What is reality?" I realized that, for the first time in my life, I was questioning life and doubting my old beliefs. I continued my writing.

"Am I going to accept the only reality which is that we can never be together and we will live the rest of our lives with deep bitterness and regret? Or does another kind of reality exist? For example, can I create the beautiful vision my heart and soul have always been longing for?"

My heart felt lighter when thinking in this brand new way and I decided to go even further.

"Dear God, I am in deep unbearable pain, the pain of separation. You have clearly noticed this. I need to find a way out! So, please help me! Help us! If Your divine will is to let me and my beloved Oskar stay together, then, please show me the way! Reveal the path!"

I used all my will power and strength to write down those words. Feeling exhausted, I then fell asleep.

The following day, when I was working on my day shift at the reception, a young lady from Australia checked in around noon. According to procedure, I asked for her passport for copying purposes.

My heart lurched! Her visa was applied for from Copenhagen! That meant she had stayed in Denmark!

I immediately wanted to ask her so many questions. But I forced myself to calm down, realizing that I should probably wait a little bit first.

Next day, I was working on my night shift. The lady came into

The Twin Flame Lover of China and Denmark

my reception and asked me some questions regarding tours and subway systems, etc. I knew it was the right moment for me to ask my questions.

"Catherine, yesterday I noticed that your visa was applied for in Copenhagen, Denmark. Were you having a holiday in Denmark, or what? How do you feel about the country? I have been thinking about visiting Denmark recently and I really would love to know more details about that country. Do you mind telling me something about it?"

Catherine: "Oh, sure, it's my pleasure. No, I wasn't traveling or studying there. In fact, I had been working there as an au pair. I lived together with a local Danish family in Copenhagen for half a year. I had my own bedroom, free food, etc. In turn I did some housework for them and sometimes I took care of the children as well. In my free time I often went out exploring the city and meeting new friends. I really like Denmark a lot..."

DeDe: "What? Excuse me, what is an au pair? How did you get such a job? Can you explain more?"

Catherine: "Sure, an au pair is..."

From that moment on, my heart could no longer be peaceful again.

For the next few days, I excitedly checked all relevant information about au pair jobs. How happy I was! I realized it was exactly the perfect opportunity I was deeply, deeply longing for! I had finally captured the magical scent of my dream!

However, I quickly denied it by thinking, "No... it is impossible to go to Denmark. How and where can I find a Danish host family? It sounds very frustrating! Besides, I do not know anyone there. It is a completely foreign land to me. It is a very big risk! I fear the unknown! I had better not be insane but behave normally. I now have finally found my dream, but sometimes it is safer just to bury our dreams deep down and not bother with the unnecessary fuss..."

How quickly my dream had come, how quickly it had gone.

The Twin Flame Lover of China and Denmark

A few days later, Catherine checked out. Before she left, she gave me some gifts, including snacks and drinks and a book titled *The Alchemist* by Paulo Coelho.

She said to me, "DeDe, this wonderful book has influenced me a lot. I've read it a few times and I still keep it because it means a lot to me. It totally changed the way I perceive things and it transformed my whole life. I hope it will also inspire you and help you make your dream come true."

I was simply startled. Two weeks ago an Australian artist named Matt also said the same thing about this book to me. He had strongly recommended I read it!

Merely coincidence or was it something meant to be?

I couldn't figure it out. I hesitated and I put the book away.

One week later, I felt deeply drawn to read the book. After reading the very first page, I didn't want to put it down. Three days later, I finished reading the whole book. After that my mind was not the same any more. Sitting alone on the terrace of our hotel, I started to reflect.

"Paulo Coelho is a truly great writer. I wish I could speak as wisely as he writes! He writes with his soul and he speaks directly to my soul! He reveals the very truth about love and life! He writes about dreams, love, courage, magic, spirit, legends. They are all resonating with me! A long, long time ago I wished to hear words like that. I wished someone could write a book like that! And he just did it!

"He says that each one of us has our own unique talents and gifts waiting to be explored and fulfilled, that we all have our personal legends to make; he says that God has already put some magical omens along our path. If we have the courage to follow the signs, we will eventually realize our dreams; he also says that we should always listen to our hearts, because wherever our hearts are, there we will find our treasure!"

"I now see the whole picture. Matt, Catherine, Paulo Coelho, being an au pair, and this book, *The Alchemist*, are all the magical omens placed by God along my path. My dream is to go to Denmark and it is very likely that I will find my treasure there!"

The heart understood everything. But my mind didn't want to accept or believe it, because it was used to playing the game of fear and worry.

I simply put the book away and decided to be normal.

STAGE FOUR

The Runner and the Chaser (August 2011-January 2013)

Nothing except pure love and light cannot stand between the Twin Flames. Heavy emotional baggage, egoistic thinking, and acting patterns need to be cleared out in order to let Divine Love grow and flourish between them... The seemingly deeply hurtful emotions and unbearable pain each twin is experiencing at this stage serves not only for the purposes of testing and strengthening their spirit, but also helps each to search for their higher self for healing and further soul growth...

Chapter 13

The Soul Level Abandonment From Me to You

Three months went by and I heard nothing from you. On the one hand I felt relieved about it, because it meant I didn't need to deal with my worries and confusions any more. But on the other hand, I was deeply disappointed and I started to fear I had truly lost you.

By the beginning of July, I could not bear it any more. I decided to write to you and find out what was going on with you.

Sitting alone on our hotel's terrace, I spent approximately two hours writing a loving email to you, in which I confessed about my deep regrets and my sincere wish for us to be together again.

My intuition told me it didn't feel right to do it. However, I persisted, because I simply couldn't bear the pain of missing you any more.

After sending the email, I felt rather anxious and unsettled. I feared I had done the wrong thing. I decided to go out for a bike ride to ease my restless emotions. But it didn't make me feel any better. Instead, I felt more restless. I didn't know how to calm myself down and I started to lose control. I was riding wildly!

"Ouch! That hurts!"

I got hit by another bike I hadn't noticed and I fell to the ground. My right knee was bleeding and I could see the raw flesh inside. All I felt was pain. But it didn't really matter. My very first thought was, "This is a very bad sign! I doubt whether Oskar's reply will cause me as much pain as this!"

The Twin Flame Lover of China and Denmark

A few minutes later, I started to ride back, with a painful right knee and a suffering heart.

As soon as I arrived at my dormitory, I opened my email and saw that you had replied.

You said you had already let go of our love and had moved on! You wished me to move on, too!

I couldn't believe what I was reading and I completely froze. The way you wrote, your words and the cold energy that could be felt emanating from the words, all felt so distant and hurtful. I didn't understand and I desperately wanted to know why!

So I wrote you an email like this, "Oskar, in your email you came across quite cold and official, as if I was a stranger to you. I feel so sad about this! You have completely changed into another person! Why? What happened?"

A few days later, I received a rather long email from you. Before reading it, I took my computer to our hotel's terrace where I could be alone, so that I wouldn't be disturbed. You wrote, "Dear DeDe, I am sorry if I came across cold and distant in my previous email. Please forgive me! I never meant to hurt your feelings or emotions.

"Before writing this email to you, I thought about it many times, wondering whether I should or should not, because I know it will be a big risk for me to tell you all of this. I don't know what your reactions will be... But still, I want to be honest with you by telling you everything I have experienced during the past few months.

"You asked me not to contact you any more. We broke up again, when I thought we would stay together. After that, I felt very low and sad. I totally lost myself in thinking about you almost every day. It seemed as if there was no other way to cure my pain. So I listened to the stupid saying, 'The quickest way to forget about the old love is to embrace a new love.' So I decided to move on and start a new relationship with someone else.

"Afterwards, I met a girl whom I found fascinating. We went out together a few times. It was interesting at the beginning but it only lasted for one week, because I discovered that my heart was still missing you. You are the only one I truly love! I want to be with you!

"As you know, soon I will have a two-months' summer holiday. I already booked my flight ticket to India to visit my friend Pascal. And I was thinking, if you like, can I come to Beijing to see you afterwards? I miss you so much.

"Waiting for your reply, my love.

"Yours, Oskar."

It was a beautiful sunny warm day, flowers were blooming and birds were singing. However, after reading your email, I felt as if it had turned into a dark, cold, rainy day. All I felt was unspeakable pain, sorrow and anger. I was deeply hurt and sobbed uncontrollably.

You had dated another girl! You had just caused me the most intolerable pain!

I considered your action wrong and stupid; I grieved that you could betray our love so easily; I judged you as unfaithful and lacking in loyalty. I concluded you deserved the cruelest punishment from me.

For a few seconds I wanted to forgive you and even ask you to come back, because I still loved you deeply. However, my feelings of hurt outweighed my willingness to forgive. As much love as had once been between us, there now was anger. All I wanted to do was to get my revenge.

I decided to abandon you by exiling you from my love forever, so that our suffering could become equal and my hurtful emotions could become compensated. Therefore, I wrote an extremely cold email to you.

"Dear Oskar, this will be the last email from me to you. I appreciate your honesty and your willingness to return. However, we are now finished forever. I never want to hear from you again. Please respect yourself, and do not ever contact me again. Take care."

After that, I continued sobbing bitterly, not wanting to imagine or care how hurt you would feel after reading my email.

Chapter 14

You Run Away, I Run Around

My mind was bruised and my heart was broken. I felt low and lonely. I couldn't understand why life had become an impossible dream and love had become unreachable. I was living in darkness and I longed for the light.

The only thing I felt drawn to do was to read. Deep down, a well had been opened. I desperately wanted to know more truths about love and life. Therefore, I bought all Paulo Coelho's books and started my inner searching journey.

One book after another, I felt I was being transformed and I started to ask some serious questions, like, "Who am I? Who do I want to become? Why did I come into this world? What is the meaning of my life? What is my higher purpose and mission?"

So many times I wrote down the following words in my diary, while sobbing crying at the same time.

"Dear God, please listen to me carefully. I am not living the life I truly want to. I must tell you that I desperately want to find my other half and live a happy and fulfilling life. Besides, I must figure out what my divine life work is. I need to discover my unique talents and gifts and then utilize them fully. I must wake them up and let them shine! I want a beautiful life with love, light, meaning, and abundance!"

I kept reading and writing; meanwhile, I was waiting to see if you would email me or not. Deep down, I expected you to contact me and ask for my forgiveness. I even thought that if you did, I would give us another chance. However, three months went by with no word from you. I was paralyzed. I started to regret the stupid punishment I had inflicted upon you.

One day, I felt I just couldn't suffer any more and, without thinking too much, I sent you an email and asked how you had been doing.

You replied, "Thank you for your regards. I don't really know why you are writing this email to me. But I think I need to tell you clearly that I have already moved on with my life. I have been doing fine here.

"There are times when you still automatically come into my mind. Sometimes you stay there for a few days, sometimes you do not. I don't know. Maybe I still love you in some way. But I don't really feel the need to be with you any more. I am sorry. I hope you can also move on with your life. This is the best for both of us."

You! Runner! Sudden change! Forgetting! Moving on!

Me! Stayer! Shock! Choke! Hurt! Pain!

I couldn't believe what I was reading. I was too fragile to reply. A vivid mental picture came to my mind: you were running away from me, with your strong determination and intense confusion.

Consequently, life felt even more miserable to me. Every day, I felt as if I was being torn apart by severe pain and sorrow. With all my will and strength, I wrote, "God! I can't live like this any more! I need a big change! I want a new life and a new self!"

Change was on its way, triggered by an unexpected quarrel.

Three days later, five minutes before I finished my work, I had a rather unpleasant argument with one of our managers due to some trivial matter. He felt he was not being respected, whereas I thought I was being mistreated. We concluded there was no way to work together peacefully together from that moment on.

With anger and sorrow, I ran to our hotel's terrace and cried bitterly there.

In despair, I asked life, "Why have you treated me like this? Why did you let my beloved Oskar run away? I feel he still loves me! You've driven me to the extreme point where I can find no way out and I feel like dying now! What do you want me to do? I don't want to live with this pain any more! It's too much!"

I decided to escape from my miserable life as quickly as possible.

The very next day, I quit my job without any hesitation and I put in a seven day notice. My boss Oliver knew what had happened and he understood my feelings. He asked me to stay and comforted me by saying that things would improve. However, I was totally blinded by my pain and all I wanted to do was to run, run away from everything I simply couldn't bear or understand.

Eight days later, I arrived at Lhasa, Tibet, aiming to forget about everything by traveling.

Initially, I felt quite excited and fresh about the totally different environment I was in. I even thought I might have made the right decision. However, when I found myself continually staring at your picture for a long time and when I realized you were still in my heart, I completely broke down. The truth was, I still loved you.

My au pair dream had remained unfulfilled; the pain was still there. I hadn't succeeded in running away from anything. Ten days later, it was time to go back to Beijing, as I had promised my new boss before I had left.

Beijing He Yuan International Youth Hostel would be my new workplace. I would work as an English speaking receptionist there, which I had already planned after quitting my job at the Double Happiness Courtyard Hotel. My new boss, Mr. Tan, welcomed my joining the team and held high expectations of me.

Why did I find a hostel to work for instead? Because I fooled myself by thinking that I might perhaps find my happiness back in a youth hostel. This is because I had found love and happiness while I was working at the P. Loft Youth Hostel.

I simply had no will or courage to move forward, because I believed my dream and my love were all impossible to fulfill. I would rather fall and walk backwards, so that at least I would somehow feel some sort of security by hanging on to the old way, even though it

The Twin Flame Lover of China and Denmark

was already worn out and no longer satisfying.

I forced myself to appreciate my new job and my new co-workers. However, it didn't work out. No matter how hard I tried, I just couldn't feel any passion for or connection with the job and the people. I decided to leave.

On the third day after my arrival, I told the truth to Mr. Tan and sincerely apologized. He felt disappointed to hear that. But still, he respected my decision and wished me good luck.

The following day, I left the hostel and took the train back home—the only place I could think of going to.

Days at home were not necessarily happy or fulfilling. My parents' loving care warmed me up to some extent, but I was still deeply saddened by the same questions: "Why did my beloved Oskar run away from me? Why? I feel he still loves me!"

Different thoughts came to my mind.

"My feelings are wrong! He doesn't love me anymore! Or else, he wouldn't run away! Who would run away from true love? Forget about it and move on? I shouldn't hang myself from the same old tree; there are plenty of other fish in the sea!

"Maybe he still loves me, but perhaps not that much. First love will rarely work out, especially when it is a long distance international love. Perhaps I should be strong and move on toward a new love.

"He might have his own troubles and problems. He's still a student and he doesn't yet have the ability to make this difficult love work out. Indeed, we have some extreme obstacles to overcome. It is really quite impossible. I should simply keep this beautiful memory locked away in my heart and try to forget about it. Time will heal my wounds and teach me how to let go."

Those thoughts made some sense to me to varying degrees. However, when I genuinely thought of moving on and forgetting about you, I became totally inert. I didn't want to do it and I became convinced that I could never let you go.

Still expecting to hear nothing, I received an email from you. Writing as an "old friend," you informed me that your parents were going to attend an international medical conference in Holland and that your sister had just given birth to her first baby named Alfred. You also wrote about your busy painting days and that you had recently been preparing for your graduation. At the end, you asked how I had been doing and how were my parents and my sister.

I felt quite joyful to hear from you after such a long silence. But I was also saddened by the fact that all of a sudden, you had become an "old friend." I preferred it when you were my beloved, darling Oskar before!

I wrote back and explained that my parents had been doing well and that I was looking for a new job. In the end, I still couldn't help asking you the question, "What are your feelings about us?"

As I predicted, you confirmed that you had already moved on and that we had better just be friends.

I was torn to pieces and didn't reply.

For the following days, I wished for God to quietly take me away.

But no, She/He did not want to do that. Instead, I received a magical dream: It was quite early in the morning. I had my toothbrush and toothpaste and I was on the way to brush my teeth. Then, I somehow found myself walking to my middle school's playground. At first there was nothing there, but just a few seconds later, many big trees suddenly appeared. They were mystical, ancient trees with strong roots and evergreen leaves. Each was unique and special. I recognized that they were the awakened trees with a high level of intelligence and awareness I had dreamed of before. They were full of power and strength!

I was astonished to be in their presence and I seemed to receive their powerful energies of hope and light that they were transmitting to me.

A moment later, a taller tree with evergreen leaves appeared and I noticed that there was a beautiful sunrise slowly appearing from behind the mystical tree!

I woke up and I could still clearly remember the entire dream. I was surprised, but I also felt energized.

As usual, I went to the website called *www.dreammoods.com* to check the prophetic meaning of my dream.

"To see evergreen trees in your dream signifies wealth, happiness, immortality, high aspirations, and knowledge. The dream represents the cycle of life and may be trying to offer you hope in the midst of despair.

To see the sunrise in your dream represents new beginnings, renewal of life and energy, and fulfillment of your goals and purpose. You are about to embark on a new adventure in your personal life."

Those words felt so cheerful and uplifting to me. Even though I had doubts about them, it did not alter the fact that I began to feel better and I decided to move forward.

With my former co-worker Vivian's help, I found a similar job in Michael's House Hotel in Beijing. Because of my working experience and Vivian's reference, an interview was not needed and I could join the team as soon as I would return to Beijing.

With a new job offer, I felt quite relieved. I packed my luggage, said farewell to my parents and took the train.

Chapter 15

Return to Double Happiness Courtyard Hotel

On December 24th, 2011, I arrived at Michael's House and started my new job. My work duties were more or less the same as they had been at the Double Happiness Courtyard Hotel. Seven days later I was able to work independently. I told myself to forget about my old hotel and my old love and to only focus on the present and the future. However, I failed to comply with my own instructions.

Within only two weeks I started to miss the Double Happiness Courtyard Hotel. I thought about my beloved terrace, my friend Alan, and the liveliness and joy introduced by our guests. I asked myself why I would only learn to cherish something after it was gone; I regretted having quit my job and I wished a miracle could give me back my previous position.

Thinking rationally, I concluded that this could never happen. I continued working and living with an unfulfilled heart.

The au pair dream was still echoing in my heart. I took notice of it and started to actively search for further information. Finally, from the official website of the Danish Immigration Office, I discovered that in order to become an au pair, I needed to have a birth certificate and, most importantly, to find a Danish host family.

I felt quite happy about my discoveries and I immediately registered myself on some relevant au pair websites, aiming to find a Danish host family.

However, no matter how many self-introduction letters I sent out, I still heard nothing. I felt quite discouraged and dejected. I doubted if it was indeed God's will for me to go to Denmark. I was caught between giving up and continuing searching.

Somehow, around the middle of March, I contacted and asked you how you were doing. You replied that you were still busy with your graduation, that you needed to finish some paintings before the deadline. You also said that a girl in your school had conducted an interesting survey about happiness the previous week. You were asked when was the last time you felt genuinely happy.

"Last time when I was with you," you said. That was your reply to the survey.

I immediately cried out, but I didn't let you know that this was my reaction. I didn't tell you that if I were asked the same question, my answer would be the same. Because after all, you only wanted to be friends, so I kept my silence.

You also told me that during those days when we were not in touch, you wanted very much to know how I was doing, so you had typed my full name into a Google search and you were quite surprised to find my au pair profile on some websites.

I was astonished to hear what you were saying! I asked you what you thought about my plan to become an au pair.

You replied, "It sounds too risky. I don't think it's..."

This was just the kind of disappointing answer I had foreseen. I judged you to be lacking in courage and fearful of taking on responsibilities, without ever thinking that your reaction could be caused by your concern about me, instead of yourself. You probably already knew that life as an au pair might not necessarily prove to be enjoyable or fulfilling to me. You didn't want me to encounter any grievances, so you rejected the idea immediately. Was that right?

Since I didn't get a supportive answer from you, I decided to totally give up on the whole idea.

After that conversation, we talked again two or three more times, but then our contact somehow petered out again.

The Twin Flame Lover of China and Denmark

In mid-April we were told that Michael's House would temporarily close from May to July due to necessary renovation work. This didn't sound encouraging to me. I started to worry where I should go and what I wanted to do for the following two months.

However, call it fate or whatever, but this is what happened. My friend Alan contacted me, saying, "Hey DeDe, do you want to come back to Double Happiness to work again? One of the reception managers is leaving on May first. We have been looking for a competent person to take her position, but without any luck. Oliver has been asking me if I knew where you are working now. They want you to come back. What do you say? Do you want me to tell them you are here?"

DeDe: "No, no, not really. I do in fact really want to come back. But somehow, I think I will feel rather embarrassed if I return. After all, I had such an unpleasant quarrel with one of the managers there."

Alan: "Come on, don't worry. He has already forgotten the incident and he even said that he regretted it. If you come back, everyone will be happy to see you!"

DeDe: "Okay... let's try. You can tell them I am here."

Two days later, I received a phone call from Oliver's wife, Yan. She asked me how I had been doing and invited me for lunch the next day. I immediately knew what she was going to propose and I felt excited about it.

That same night, I thought to myself, "Yes! I will go back! I feel something is calling me there, there are some invisible forces attracting me to go back. Even though I cannot now see the reasons, I always remember the golden rule: listen to your heart!"

Next day, we had a delicious lunch and a lovely conversation, during which the right decision was made. My heart rejoiced and it was time to go home!

Chapter 16

I Became a Chaser

On April 30th, 2012, I came back to the Double Happiness Courtyard Hotel. The next day, I started to work. After losing my job once before, I had finally learned how to wholeheartedly appreciate the fact that I had a job. I told myself that I would work diligently and cherish everything I had, that I would never think about the impossible au pair dream or my painful love any more.

I tried very hard to forget everything and move on. However, I couldn't do it. Every morning after waking up I felt as if I was dead, that I was living my life in a tomb where passion and dreams were completely out of reach. I started to fiercely debate with myself. I wondered what exactly I should do in order to feel alive!

I thought about those charming brave young ladies in Paulo Coelho's books, whose names were Brida, Veronica, Maria and Athena. They all pursued their dreams and fulfilled themselves. Deep down, I wished I could act like those women who fought fearlessly for their dreams and their love, who dared to challenge fate and reality.

But yet, I was still waiting, waiting for nothing, in pain and desperation.

Suddenly, one day toward the end of May, I realized I couldn't hold on anymore; it was time to take action and to be brave.

I thought to myself, "I can't live my life like this any more. I can't just sit here and bear this unbearable pain. I need an answer from

Oskar! I want to chase him; I can't give up! I will do whatever I can to realize my au pair dream! I am going to fight for our destiny and change our future! Yes! I am going to be a crazy chaser! For love! For my dream! This is something I must do and I will do it!"

After that, I made many phone calls to inquire how to obtain a birth certificate. I was told it could be easily done. I felt quite happy to hear this, because initially I had imagined it was a rather complicated procedure.

The last important step, but the most difficult one, was to find a Danish host family. My Australian friend Linda helped me to rewrite my au pair profile in English. After that, I emailed my profile to many Danish families online. However, I heard nothing.

Feeling frustrated, I struggled. "What is the problem? Why can't I find a Danish host family? It's like the untouchable moon in the water! Why? How can I make it become a reality?

In Paulo Coelho's book *The Alchemist*, he says that when we truly want something, the whole universe conspires to help us achieve it. I do believe that is true. "I very much want to go to Denmark, but why is the universe not helping me at all? Is it because deep down I don't truly want this? Perhaps... I am still afraid and I obviously do not yet wholeheartedly desire this.

"And so, if my desire to realize my dream becomes a burning desire, will the universe then help me out? Yes, this should be the missing ingredient. Thus, everything has become quite clear. I should use all my will power to call upon something to happen, something which will transform my thoughts and emotions; something that will make me want to go to Denmark with a 100% dedicated heart! After that, the miracle I seek will somehow appear."

I never imagined it would be you who would make that something happen.

More or less one week later, you contacted me, asking how I was doing. You told me that you had recently got to know a very talented Danish artist, that you two liked each other very much, and that her son would visit Beijing shortly. You asked if I would like to show him around during my days off.

I said yes. You then gave my email address to the artist's son— Benjamin— and proposed that we contact each other.

I felt excited about Benjamin's arrival, not only because he was referred by you, but also because I wanted so much to ask him many questions about my dreamland, Denmark.

Two weeks later, I picked up Benjamin from the airport. He was a 20-year-old young Danish man with a lovely face and a lively spirit.

During the following days, in the company of my friend Alan, the three of us went to the Great Wall and visited several other places in Beijing. All the time, I was asking Benjamin various questions about Denmark. Like the butterfly effect, Benjamin's sudden appearance triggered something deep inside of me.

One afternoon, after Benjamin and I had visited the Summer Palace, I heard my heart crying out, "Yes! I am going to Denmark! I must go to Denmark! There is no way for me to give it up or let it go! I am still thinking crazily about my Oskar and Denmark. God, I now want it with my entire heart and soul!"

A few minutes later, it occurred to me to put the word China into the advanced search bar to see whether there were any Danish families looking for au pairs from China. Luckily, I found one and I immediately sent my introduction letter to them.

After two days of anxiously waiting, I received a reply from them. They wrote that including me they had found three candidates from China. They would do an Internet interview with each person and then decide which one they would choose. In the end, we agreed that three days later we would have the online interview.

I felt unsettled; I worried that I might not be chosen.

As I feared, the interview did not go well. The atmosphere felt rather uncomfortable and full of tension. My intuition told me I would not be chosen.

Indeed, three days later, I received their email saying they had chosen someone else.

Feeling disappointed, I immediately dissolved into tears of sadness.

"The two hardest tests on the spiritual road are the patience to wait for the right moment and the courage not to be disappointed with what we encounter." (Paulo Coelho) I found light and strength in Paulo's wise words. But even so, it didn't alter the fact that I was depressed, due to the perceived failure of my dream.

Not really knowing what to do, I often went to Paulo Coelho's official blog to find inspirational quotes.

"The world only gets better, because people risk something to make it better." Paulo was encouraging me to take the risk of going to Denmark!

"Follow your dreams, even if that includes going through some nightmares." Even though I was told no, I still needed to pursue my dream!

"If you think adventure is dangerous, try routine. It is lethal." I desperately wanted to have my own adventure!

"Dreams are not negotiable." Yes! Indeed!

"Be brave, take risks. Nothing can be a substitute for experience." Yes! I shall be brave!

"The secret of life, though, is to fall seven times, and to get up eight times." Yes! I have only fallen once; should I get up again?

"It's the possibility of having a dream come true that makes life interesting." Yes! Right! But how could I make my dream come true?

Paulo's words were inspiring and uplifting. I printed those quotes out on cards and put them on the wall, inside the closet and around the mirror in my room. In that way I could see them as often as possible, so that I could remind myself that I still had a very important dream which needed to be fulfilled.

However, many days went by and still, nothing happened. I decided to quit for a while and I started to read. Inspired by Paulo

The Twin Flame Lover of China and Denmark

Coelho's books *Brida* and *The Witch of Portobello*, I developed an interest in the areas of energy healing and human transformation. I wanted so much to learn about the esoteric world and I started to search for some information about it.

One day, I accidently found an interesting website created by an English writer named Jack. I downloaded some materials from the website and I started to read them day by day.

In one of the chapters Jack wrote, "What is reality? Reality is in fact something you can shape and create by your very thoughts and actions. Since the very dawn of time, the truth has remained this way. Everything in this universe has its own energy, energy and matter can be mutually transformed. Your thoughts are the energy, whereas your reality is the matter. Intensify and strengthen the energy of your thoughts, and magically, you will be guided to receive what you want..."

Jack's wise words removed many walls of impossibility from my mind. The light of truth began to shine through. From that moment on, I believed my dream would come true and I stood up again with hope and faith.

A few days later, I received an inner urge suggesting that I should modify my au pair profile in a new way. More specifically, it prompted me to reorganize my words by focusing on introducing myself sincerely and explaining what I could offer the family as an au pair, instead of what I wanted to receive.

I never had any confidence in my writing ability, but following my urge was something of extreme importance. I decided to bring my inner wise writer out. After three hours of thinking and modifying, a rather warm au pair letter finally emerged.

"The reasons why I want to be an au pair: I want to broaden my cultural horizons, to see and experience how things are like in a totally different place, to dream and explore, to fulfill and introduce more color to my life.

"My interests: I enjoy reading inspiring books and writing

The Twin Flame Lover of China and Denmark

down my inner thoughts. I have an intense passion for flowers and gardening. I feel very connected and joyful when I am close to nature, especially forests. I am very good at English, singing, dancing, interacting with people, as well as having a sense of humor. I also like swimming, drawing, art and traveling.

"Dear Family:

"My full name is Defang Wan; it sounds similar to "Wonderful." DeDe is my nick name, which I like.

"The reasons why I want to be an au pair in Denmark: I worked as an English speaking receptionist in an international youth hostel in Beijing for a few months in 2009. There, I had the wonderful and great experience of meeting young travelers from all over the world. This experience had a great effect on me and initiated my desire to explore the world and have experiences of my own.

"Since 2010 I have been working as an English speaking reception manager at the Beijing Double Happiness Courtyard Hotel. Here I have worked daily dealing mainly with guests from European countries, interacting with them even after work. Through these unique experiences I have developed an interest in European cultures and countries.

"In 2011, I met an Australian girl who had worked as an au pair in Denmark. I was fascinated by her stories about Denmark and knew then that I wanted the same opportunities to fulfill my dream. Since then, I have been checking relevant information about Denmark. To explore its culture and people has become one of my dreams.

"What I can mainly offer: To bring some insights about my own country's culture and its people, as well as its interesting differences from yours in various forms; to cook real, authentic and delicious Chinese food for your family; to make your house clean, tidy and as beautiful as it can be; to treat your children lovingly and possibly be their little good friend.

"I do not have any au pair or nanny experiences, but I have had opportunities to interact and take care of children. For me, to talk and do activities with children feels like in a movie, because they are so honest and lovely, as well as emotionally real. I enjoyed my times with children very much and I look forward to experiencing more on a deeper level.

"I consider myself to be a very honest, responsible and lively person with a loving heart and wonderful life spirit, with a great deal to offer. I am excited to realize my au pair dream and I look forward to hearing from you in the near future.

Warm Regards,

DeDe."

I was satisfied with this new version. My heart smiled.

The very next second, a Danish family's profile suddenly caught my eye. Looking at their profile picture, I thought to myself, "This family looks like a genuinely happy one, especially the mother; I feel I have met her before..."

I felt a strange urge to open their profile, so I did. While I was reading their profile I was talking to myself like this: "This family lives in a village called Farup in the town of Ribe, the oldest town in Denmark. It's a very idyllic place with flowers, a pebble road and beautiful houses. They have two boys named Sofus and Tobias; one is seven and the other is five. I will need to do some housework for them. I should be quite good at speaking English. I am expected to come from an interesting country with a different culture, such as this country and that country, and China!"

My intuition told me it was the right family. I re-read their description and immediately sent my new au pair letter to them.

The following day, I received a long warm email from them, including their detailed family introduction and the town websites for Ribe and Esbjerg.

They wrote that they were building their new house at the moment, and that it would be finished by December. If everything went well, I was expected to arrive at the beginning of January. They also asked me when I would have time to have a chat with them online, saying that if we both felt right, I would be their next au pair.

I felt excited to hear that! I couldn't believe that the miracle I longed for was happening!

As planned, the following Saturday, I logged into Skype and got to see the father Thomas, the mother Mette, and the two lovely boys Sofus and Tobias.

I couldn't remember what exactly was said except that we felt happy to see each other and there was a sense of acceptance and warmth in our conversation. In the end, as I expected and hoped, I was chosen!

The impossible was finally transformed into reality. I was ecstatic with joy, broadcasting my happiness to the whole world!

Chapter 17

The Days Before Going to Denmark

During the whole of August, I was running around to collect all the necessary documents; I was also interviewed at the Danish Embassy. Finally, at the beginning of September, all I needed to do was wait for two, three, or more months, to know whether the visa would be issued or not.

At that point, I was struggling with myself regarding whether I should tell you I was coming to Denmark or not. In the end, I wrote you an email, asking your thoughts about our love and my au pair plan. Your answer was still the same: you had already moved on, to be an au pair was too risky.

I was devastated and I concluded it was the right decision to not tell you I was most probably coming to Denmark.

Life and work continued as before, except that I started to bring two new rituals into my life. One was that every evening after I finished my work, I would go to our hotel's terrace, and dance there for fifteen minutes, without any music and with my eyes closed.

I decided to do this, simply because of the book *Brida* by Paulo Coelho. In the book, Brida was told by her master, Wicca: "The Earth we are living in is a divine lively being with her own soul and spirit. Every moment she is communicating with us by sending her energy to us on her unique frequency.

"All you need to do is listen, listen with your heart and soul. Close your eyes, you don't need to know any movements or steps; as long as you listen and believe, you will be guided by a higher force. You will know how to follow its hidden rhythm to dance. Doing so, your innate power and potential will be activated and woken up."

I was fascinated by Wicca's teaching and I started to follow it. At the beginning, everything felt so awkward and difficult, especially since I had never danced before. I laughed at myself a lot and thought I was being rather weird. But still, I persevered.

More or less one month later, things began to flow. I suddenly knew how to move my hands and feet naturally. I discovered that I especially liked using my hands to draw small and large circles in the air. It felt very strange, but also familiar to me, as if I was picking up some forgotten skills I had before.

As I continued practicing, my hands were transformed, they had somehow become alive and sensitive to energy. My palms felt warm and special, as if there was electricity flowing inside them.

I felt shocked and excited about all these changes. In order to figure out what exactly was happening, I started to read books about chakras and healing. I concluded that my hand chakra was opening. Perhaps I was awakening my healing ability. But in order to become a real healer, much training and practice were needed. I had a long way to go...

The second ritual was that every night before I went to bed I would always meditate for about fifteen minutes. I felt my heart was not suffering in pain but bathing in peace and light during those precious moments.

These two important rituals began playing a crucial role in my life. They offered me much strength and power. I told myself that no matter what happened in my life, I would never stop practicing.

Working, reading, thinking, writing, dancing, meditating, feelings of restlessness and excitement... Time flew and, after nearly three months of anxious waiting, on December 16th, 2012, my au pair visa was issued. My heart and spirit rejoiced.

When this happened, I wrote a resignation letter to my manager, Oliver. In it I expressed my gratitude for his support and trust in me, also my strong resolve to follow my dream and path.

Oliver said that as a manager, he felt regretful because my leaving was a loss to the hotel. But personally he encouraged me to go forward and to experience the new me. He added that whenever I returned, I would be more than welcome to work in the hotel again.

With his blessing, I left the Double Happiness Courtyard hotel on the January 7th, 2013.

I then spent one week with my best friend, and another week at home with my parents. My flight to Denmark was in the early morning of of January 23rd. I returned to Beijing on the 21st.

Before I left for the airport, I looked through the diaries I had written, remembering all my deep longings and yearnings.

"May my wishes come true, may my heart be proud and filled with ecstasy, may my life's wheel begin to turn to another page; from there a truly loving, powerful, confident, wonderful new self will arise.

"To the inner divine Goddess who always resides within me, please show me the way, teach me how to put my faith in you, let me become fully who I was born to be, help me remember that I am free, that I have infinite power to choose and create. You—the divine Goddess—are the woman who I want to become. I name you She.

"She lived in ancient times inside of me and is a part of me. I deeply adore her, for she feels so gentle, kind and sweet. She is truly loving and joyful, just like a beautiful sunflower. Yet she is so powerful and wise, she knows how to communicate with the stars and the angels.

"Her power comes from deep within. This is reflected in her ever sustained confidence that simply by being her true self she will always bring her love back. Eventually, they will find each other and be together, till the end of time.

"Her shining spirit will help her survive the hardest times, till she finds and follows her path. Afterwards, she will be with light, become the light and will continue to shine.

"Her love and her profound understanding will help her fulfill her soul's mission. When she dies among the lovely flowers, she will smile with the greatest sense of satisfaction. With deep compassion and love, she will serenely flow to her next divine journey.

"We are the master of our destiny, the captain of our soul.

"Dear spirits, may I have your divine love and guidance."

STAGE FIVE

Surrender of the Heart
(January 2013-December 2013)

The chaser is totally crushed at a certain point, when she tries to run away from healing herself. However, it also marks the beginning of the twin's journey of becoming an illuminated human. The runner will continue running in order to grow and develop further in his own way, which also sets up the boundary for the chaser's higher good of achieving evolution and higher states of consciousness... This is a divinely designed time to demonstrate their faith and exercise oneself to become a qualified light worker of the Great Creator...

Chapter 18
Arriving in Copenhagen, Denmark

About 1 a.m., January, 23rd, 2013, I got on a plane from Beijing to Brussels, from where I was scheduled to change to my flight to Copenhagen. All the way, I was feeling strange, as if I was living in a dream. Everything happening around me felt unbelievable and unreal.

Next day at 7 a.m. I arrived at Brussels airport; seeing so many westerners walking and talking around me, I felt more awe and excitement. Only two hours later, I would see my dreamland—Denmark!

I turned on the music of my favorite movie *Kiki's Delivery Service* by Hayao Miyazaki, immersing myself in the lovely music and the wonderful feeling that I was doing the same thing Kiki did in the movie: realizing her dream. I felt magically happy and proud.

From the plane window I could see the ocean, the land, and the vague images of the houses down below. My heart couldn't help beating wildly. What a feeling that was! I had finally arrived in Denmark!

Copenhagen airport was relatively small compared with Beijing International Airport. I easily followed the signs and walked toward the exit.

I spotted a lovely Danish couple waving and smiling at me. They were Ane and Harold from Copenhagen, whom I had met at the Double Happiness Courtyard Hotel in 2011. I would stay in their house for the following two nights. After that, I would take the train to Mette and Thomas's house.

The Twin Flame Lover of China and Denmark

Ane and Harold asked me if I would like to take a drive with them around the central area of Copenhagen before driving to their house. I was excited to accept their generous offer.

Copenhagen seemed to be a charming city. I saw many colorful buildings, lovely Danish style flower shops, bread shops, and clothing shops. I felt as if I was in one of Miyazaki's movies!

However, all these beautiful sensations couldn't prevent the fact that I was feeling dizzy and tired due to jetlag. I felt rather unsettled physically and emotionally; I did not feel centered and my head was spinning with all these new impressions.

After the city tour, we arrived at Ane and Harold's house.

When I saw their typical Danish house with lovely furniture, vases and candle holders, their fully equipped kitchen and all the flowers in the house, my feelings of awe kept increasing. Again, I felt everything was just so unreal.

Ane prepared a delicious meal with lamb, fish and salad for our dinner, which we enjoyed very much. For the first time in my life, I was using a knife and fork to eat with. Ane said to me good-humoredly: "DeDe, from today on, you will have to practice using a knife and fork; no more chopsticks for you."

I agreed with her; I felt change was coming.

After the dessert, we started to chat. Ane told me that when she was 16- years-old she had gone to England and had worked there as an au pair for about eight months. She said that the experience had taught her a lot that she would never forget.

When Ane was recalling her au pair days, I somehow sensed she was worrying about me. I felt puzzled but I simply thought to myself, "I am looking forward to being an au pair; I don't think I will encounter any difficulties or problems."

The following day, we went to a shopping mall nearby. I felt excited to be there and I was quite impressed by the service of the shop assistants I encountered, who were genuinely helpful and friendly.

Ane bought me a few clothes and a green bag as a "Welcome to Denmark" gift for me. I liked all items very much and I felt grateful for Ane's loving kindness and generosity.

We came back home around 2 p.m. Shortly after that, my Danish friend Jette whom I had met at P. Loft in Beijing arrived. Jette brought me a bunch of tulips as a gift; they were very nice.

Jette stayed with us for dinner that night. We talked and enjoyed ourselves a lot. In a foreign country where I knew virtually nothing I now had trusting and supportive friends around me. I felt lucky and blessed.

I was still feeling rather tired and my head was still spinning. About 9 p.m. I started to feel sleepy. Harold told me that within one week I would feel completely normal. Then Ane gently said to me, "I know why you are here. You still cannot forget about Oskar..."

I thought to myself, "He is love. Love already exists in every cell of my body and has occupied my every thought and whole being. There is no way I can let it go. I came here for a final answer..."

Next day, on January 26th, around 10 a.m., Ane and Harold drove me to the Copenhagen Central Train Station. My train was scheduled to leave at 11 a.m. and I would be arriving at Bramming station at 3 p.m., from where Mette was supposed to pick me up.

I got on the train and we had to say our farewells.

"Dear DeDe, have a safe journey! Send us a message or an email when you arrive there. You should just see us as your old uncle and aunt in Denmark. We will do our best to support you any time you need anything. When you have time, please come and visit us. Take care!"

"I will send you an email right after I arrive there. Everything will be fine. Thank you, thank you for everything. Please go back now, it's so cold outside. We will see each other again! Take care!"

After settling myself down, I started to look through the window. All the way, I saw many forests covered by pure white snow and many typical Danish style houses. They reminded me of the beautiful fairy

The Twin Flame Lover of China and Denmark

tale *Snow White and the Seven Dwarves*. I just couldn't believe that I was really in Denmark!

Feelings of excitement overwhelmed me, but meanwhile, I started to worry, "Where is my Danish host family? What does their place look like? What are my au pair duties? How will I feel about everything there?"

Thinking about those questions, I felt uneasy. However, I cheered myself up by thinking, "No matter what, I will survive. The divine spirit will guide me. I am blessed."

Chapter 19

A Magical Dream; Contacting Oskar

I got off the train and immediately I saw Mette enthusiastically waving to me, with a few small Chinese flags in her hand. There were two young boys standing next to her. I recognized them as Sofus and Tobias. I quickened my pace and walked toward them.

They smiled and hugged me warmly. I felt excited to meet them. After that, I got in Mette's car, on my way to my new home.

I was sitting in the front seat, right next to Mette. We chatted for a while regarding our interests and likes, etc. I noticed Sofus and Tobias were both silent and staring at me curiously. I asked Mette if they were always quiet like that. Mette said: "No, not really. They will revert to their true selves when we get home."

Finally, there I was, in my new home. Sofus and Tobias quickly took off their shoes and immediately started to run around and play with each other. Like Mette said, their true selves were revealed, and I adored them both right from the start.

Mette kindly showed me around the house. Her and Thomas's bedroom was upstairs, while Sofus and Tobias shared a bedroom downstairs; my bedroom was going to be next to theirs. Mette also showed me the kitchen, bathroom, and pointed out the various utilities. It was a newly built house which had just been finished in December. So everything felt quite fresh and new. I especially liked my new bedroom which was so clean and full of light.

However, at the same time, I felt a bit apprehensive. I realized it would be the first time that I would be living with a foreign family in a foreign country. A little overcome by jetlag and my mixed emotions, I excused myself and retreated to my bedroom.

In silence, I agonised, "Why didn't I check where exactly I was heading before I came? Why did I shut myself away in this small farm village? There are very few houses nearby and all around are just some fields. Besides, the weather is really so bad..."

I was full of negative thoughts, not able to recognize that perhaps it was my soul's plan to put me in this quiet place so that I could fully concentrate on my spiritual healing and growth. Back then, all I wanted to do was to escape from a situation that I perceived as detrimental to my wellbeing. At this point all I wanted to do was to go straight back to Beijing.

Next morning Mette gave me a schedule defining my daily cleaning duties. I thought it was a very fair contract. From Monday to Friday I only needed to work three to five hours a day and I had time off during the weekend. However, when looking at the details of my cleaning duties, I felt crestfallen. "Clean the table after dinner, vacuum the floor, empty the dish washer, do the laundry, tidy the bedrooms," etc.

For the next few days I had to accustom myself to different cleaning methods and appliances, which felt awkward and even frustrating to me. My life seemed to involve a lot of drudgery.

I should have mentally prepared or imagined the 'housework' aspect of being an au pair before I came. I had not, because I had focused exclusively on my love issue. I was aware this was no one's fault but my own. I was like a deflated balloon and I began to doubt Paulo Coelho's saying "Follow your heart and transform your life, because wherever your heart is, there you will find your treasure."

Nothing made any sense to me back then, except that I remembered clearly one occult dream I had on the fourth day after my arrival. I was struggling to swim in a dark dirty river, and there were monsters chasing me. It was difficult for me to swim and to escape from these monsters. However, I desperately wanted to see Oskar who was on the other side of the river, so I tried very hard to reach him. Finally, I managed to reach land and was reunited with him. I kissed him gently, but he was speechless, suffering deep pain and confusion; at the same time I was suffering due to his silent rejection, with my heart full of fear and hurt. But then, suddenly, a path appeared. It was a spiritual path illuminated by a bright light. At the entrance to the path there was a beautiful container with flowers with light surrounding it. I started walking toward the path... and then I woke up.

Much later on I understood the prophetic meaning of this magical dream. The difficult swimming process meant that after my days as a chaser in Beijing I would finally meet Oskar and I would be rejected. After that, I would walk toward my path of becoming an enlightened human.

Back then, I wasn't aware of the significance of this dream. I struggled a lot, wondering whether I should contact you or not, because deep down I intuitively sensed the meeting was likely to make things even worse, especially when I was not only unhappy but also living in a difficult situation.

However, I still called you.

DeDe: "Hi, Oskar?"

Oskar: "Yes. Hi, DeDe? Actually, this might sound a bit weird but recently I had a feeling that you would contact me."

DeDe: Really? Are we telepathically connected? "Well, that sounds quite strange. But okay, where are you now?"

Oskar: "I am actually in my parents' house, we were eating dinner together."

DeDe: "Do you have anything special to celebrate, or what?"

Oskar: "No, no, not really. It's just that a few days ago I accidentally fell from my bike and it was a bit serious. Next Monday I am traveling to Mexico; it's a trip I have been planning for a long time and I look forward to it very much. I plan to stay there for at least five months. Before I leave I want my father to check me over. You know, he is a doctor. I just want to make sure I have no broken bones or other injuries."

I couldn't believe what I was hearing. I couldn't figure out why, but as soon as I arrived at Denmark, you were planning to leave for Mexico! I concluded it must be God's cruel plan and that She or He was simply fooling around with me. Only months later did I realize that the separation was for my higher good, which could only be achieved by experiencing a time of solitary reflection.

I held my shock in check and we continued talking.

DeDe: "Well... your Mexico trip, that sounds very interesting. You must feel very excited about it."

Oskar: "Mm... Yes, in a way I'm really looking forward to it very much. I've been spending a lot of time painting and drawing, etc. I feel I need some kind of break. So, where are you now at this moment?"

Normally, I would say: "Mm, I am in my hotel; I am walking on the street; I am lying on my bed... I am..." But at that moment I was afraid to tell you the truth and I didn't want to lie to you either. So I changed my approach.

DeDe: "Why are you asking me such a boring question now? I do not want to tell you!"

You were a bit amused by my sudden change of approach, and you laughingly said, "Come on, what's the problem? Where are you now? Tell me, please."

DeDe: "It's really a very boring question you just asked me. I am in a secret place and you would never guess where it is. But hey, there isn't enough money left in my Skype account, so I think within one or two minutes our connection will be automatically cut off."

Oskar: "I will call you back in an hour or so, if that's alright. By then, I will be back in my own studio, where I can use my computer to call you. Just keep your Skype open."

DeDe: "Okay, I'll wait."

The Twin Flame Lover of China and Denmark

After that, the connection got cut off. I felt excited and unsettled. I feared that if I told you I was in Denmark you would still tell me that you had moved on; I feared that, after hearing such news, I would have to go back to Beijing with a broken heart, which was not something I wanted at all.

"Everything happens for a reason. There has to be a divine solution to this situation!" I wrote these words in my diary while I was anxiously awaiting your phone call.

More or less one hour later, you called back. Probably you already sensed something unusual. The very first sentence you said was, "Where are you now exactly? Please tell me."

No more hiding, I decided to tell you the truth.

DeDe: "I am now in Denmark, the nearest town to this place is called Ribe. Yes, I found a Danish family to work for as an au pair. I actually arrived at Denmark on January 26th."

Deep silence followed. This was something I had predicted.

Oskar: "Well... I never imagined that you would really come to Denmark as an au pair. So, how is it?"

DeDe: "Not very good, actually. I had to do housework and soon I will have to learn Danish at the local school. I think I might go back to Beijing."

When I was saying that, I was hoping you would ask me to stay. However, as I had deeply feared, you said, "I really appreciate that you had come so far for me. But I told you I have moved on already. I don't want to hurt you again and again..."

DeDe: (No, I don't believe you really moved on! I FEEL you still love me deeply!) "Yes, I know you have already moved on."

Oskar: "I want to see you. As an au pair, you should be free at the weekend, right? Can you come to Copenhagen this Friday?"

DeDe: "Yes, I am free during the weekends. If everything works out, if there are no accidents or delays, I can probably take the train to Copenhagen this Friday."

Oskar: "No no, there won't be any delays or accidents. I can't believe that you really are in Denmark now..."

DeDe: "So, where exactly should we meet at the train station?"

Oskar: "Right where you get off, I will be able to easily spot you."

DeDe: "Where exactly? What if I get lost?"

Oskar: "No no, you won't get lost. Our train station is very small, not as big as Beijing's. I will easily find you, don't worry."

DeDe: "Okay, fine. So, see you on Friday then."

Oskar: "Yes. See you on Friday."

I hung up the phone, my mood becoming even more complicated and more unsettled. After two years' of waiting and hoping to see you, I finally would be able to see you again.

"Are you still the same or have you changed? How will we feel? What will happen afterwards? Will you give me a big sweet hug or a small cold one? Will you..."

Two days later, on February 8th, I got on the train from Bramming to Copenhagen. All the way, a never-felt-before strange feeling overwhelmed me. I anxiously thought, "What am I heading into? Is it going to be a bright new beginning or a miserable ending?"

Chapter 20

The Final Meeting With Oskar

I got off the train and immediately saw you walking toward me. You didn't look as good as you had made yourself sound in your emails. Like me, you too seemed saddened by the separation. I sensed you had built an invisible wall around yourself, aiming to keep your distance from me. As a result, I received only a small hug.

After the "hello" and "how are you," you said, "It took me two days to digest the fact that you are now in Denmark."

I could understand that. I always loved and admired your ability to choose your words. I thought that using the word *digest* was very clever. However, I did not reply, because I did not know what to say. Destiny had put us in this situation and we had to courageously face it.

We were still walking within the train station. I told you I was hungry and thirsty, that I wanted something to eat. So we went into a cake shop we happened to be passing by. Once inside, I could see many westerners eating, drinking, talking, etc. I couldn't help thinking with some amusement and a lot of pain, "Aha! This is our first date in Denmark!"

I ordered a cake and a drink, saying that I would pay for it myself. You insisted that you would pay and you paid with your credit card.

I wanted to have my drink first, so you put my cake in your backpack. Meanwhile, realizing that my hands were suffering from the cold wind, you took off your gloves and asked me to wear them,

The Twin Flame Lover of China and Denmark

adding, "There's a small hole in one of them, I hope you don't mind. I know you like beautiful things."

I loved your gentle consideration, even though I wasn't totally sure whether it was born of love or kindness, since you had claimed that you had moved on.

DeDe: "Thank you for your gloves. So, where are we heading to? I mean, I am quite hungry and I would like something hot to eat. Do you know any restaurants with reasonable prices nearby?"

Oskar: "Mm... I don't know this area very well. But I was thinking that maybe we can go to my favorite place in Denmark? It is called Christiana. Maybe we can find a good restaurant there. But of course only if you want to go there."

DeDe: "Okay, sounds interesting, let's go. Are we walking there? How long will it take?"

Oskar: "More or less half an hour. On the way, I can tell you something about Denmark, and be your guide."

How interesting life can be. A few years ago, I introduced you to Beijing. Back then, you were telling me stories about Danish streets and buildings. Again, I felt I was living in a dream.

A few minutes before we entered Christiana, you suddenly stopped and said to me, "Didn't I tell you that I had already moved on? And why didn't you even tell me you were coming to Denmark? You really came at quite a bad time. You know, next Monday I am traveling to Mexico!"

DeDe: "You didn't like or approve of my au pair plan when I told you about it. So I came here without telling you. I didn't want to interfere in your affairs. You can still go to Mexico next Monday and enjoy your travel plans. There's no need to feel upset. I wish you a pleasant journey!"

You did not reply, and our conversation somehow petered out. A few minutes later, we were sitting in a restaurant in Christiana.

I ordered rice and vegetables, whereas you ordered spaghetti. However, I was disappointed with what I had ordered and I complained to you that the rice was the worst I had ever tasted. You immediately switched our dishes, as you explained that your noodles tasted better than my rice.

I felt grateful for your kind consideration, recalling the many loving moments we had once shared together.

However, reality pulled me back.

Oskar: "Why didn't you even let me know you are coming to Denmark? I still don't get it. Suppose I had not been in Denmark? What if I already have a girlfriend? I am going to Mexico next Monday, the day after tomorrow. Can you go to Mexico with me? Do I have to refund my flight ticket to prove that I care about you? You really came at a very bad time…"

Silently I thought, "I cannot go to Mexico with you because I have my au pair obligation to fulfill. Besides, what about the visa and the money that would be needed? I know you still care about me, but it won't change anything if you refund your ticket. And how could I have known about your crazy plan to go to Mexico?"

I asked you the only question I cared about.

DeDe: "So, do you have a girlfriend now?"

Oskar: "No, not really, except the girl I dated for seven days, which I told you about before. After that, I have not had another girlfriend. What about you?"

DeDe: "No, no one. So, after we finish here, where else are we going? You are my guide."

Oskar: "Do you want to go to my studio to see what I have been doing? Today is Friday, none of the other people are there. I can show you some of my paintings, if you would like to."

DeDe: "Yes, okay, that sounds interesting. How far is it from here?"

Oskar: "No more than 20 minutes from here. On the way, we will pass a few galleries, where I've been displaying my paintings for sale. Maybe you would like to have a look."

Hearing this, I realized you were not a student any more, but a young, talented artist who was building up his painting career. I felt happy and proud of you. But meanwhile, I couldn't help feeling sorry for myself, because I didn't know what I wanted to do with my life.

Oskar: "Look on your right hand side, can you guess what building that is?"

DeDe: "It looks very nice and modern; is it an office or something?"

Oskar: "It's a bank. A few months ago I sold them a painting."

DeDe: "Wow... how much for?"

You lowered your voice; you said: "30,000 Danish Kroner."

I was shocked, feeling even more sorry for myself.

DeDe: "That's a lot of money. Congratulations."

Oskar: "Mm... Thank you."

We soon arrived at your studio, the very same studio you used to call me from, which I fantasized about countless times, always wishing that one day I could see it with my own eyes.

Finally, there I was. It was a spacious room with your paintings hanging on the wall, an old sofa in the middle, some books on a shelf, and a small loft located right under the ceiling. There was a long ladder connecting the main studio with the loft.

DeDe: "Oskar! Is that small room your bedroom? You live up there? How did you build it?"

Oskar: "Yes, it is. My sister's boyfriend helped me build it. He is a very good carpenter. I enjoy living up there very much. I cannot only save money by not renting an apartment to live in, but I also can save a lot of time and energy. This is my living and working area."

DeDe: "It looks very interesting. Can I go up there and have a look? Please hold the ladder for me. I have never climbed such a high ladder before. I'm a bit scared."

Oskar: "Yes, of course. You can go up there now. I will hold the ladder for you."

DeDe: "Okay, but you must also climb up afterwards."

The Twin Flame Lover of China and Denmark

Oksar: "Sure, I will."

After the adventure of climbing the long ladder, there I was, right in your mini-sized bedroom, about approximately ten feet by seven feet. The very first thing that caught my eye was the big Chinese poster pinned to the wall right above your pillow.

That poster looked familiar to me. I remembered it was a gift from the farm lady whose house we stayed in for two nights in 2009.

I wondered, "Why did you put this poster here? Don't you know that it will remind you of something or someone (me)? Did you put it here on purpose? Why?"

I also noticed a small basket and a dragonfly shaped lamp hanging on the wall. They were unique and lovely. My small heart worried if these were gifts from some girls.

By that time, you had already climbed up, and you were sitting beside me.

DeDe: "This basket and that dragonfly lamp are very pretty. Who gave them to you?"

Oksar: "They are indeed very lovely. I took the basket from my parents' house and the lamp was a present from my sister."

DeDe: "That's good. So, do your parents know you are living here? What do they think about it? Did you ever invite them to this place?"

Oksar: "Yes, my parents know that I am living here. I actually asked them a few times if they would like to come here, but they never came. My mother often says that I should find a normal apartment to live in and so on... But I enjoy living here."

DeDe: "I never asked you this question before, but now I would like to know what your mother said about us, when we were still together."

Oksar: "She asked what we were planning to do together."

DeDe: "My mother also asked the same question. Okay... now I want to go down, but can you go first and then hold the ladder for me?"

Oskar: "Yes, of course."

After you came down, we sat together on the sofa, holding hands together. As always, I enjoyed your loving presence.

I wished time could stay still, that we could be close to each other, just like in that moment. But no, time was passing quickly. And I had some questions I needed to ask.

DeDe: "So, what do you say about us? You know what I mean."

Hearing this, you distanced yourself from me, your hand no longer holding mine.

Oskar: "I really appreciate it that you came to Denmark for my sake. I still care about you, or even love you. I guess there are many types of love in this world. But this kind of love is not the one that makes me want to pour out all my energy to make it work out or to settle down and have children with you. I truly feel that I have already moved on. It's totally up to you if you decide to go back to Beijing or stay here as an au pair. As you said, you can burn all the gifts or change your email address or cell phone number. It doesn't really matter to me now."

I was falling, breaking, crashing and collapsing, feeling that a kind of devastating earthquake was happening to my heart and soul. Pain, deepest soul-level pain, pain of rejection, pain of abandonment, all flooded into me.

I couldn't believe what I was hearing and I didn't know how to handle it. I had always believed that you still loved me deeply and there was no one who could take my special place in your heart.

Was that the ultimate truth of your soul or just another delusion?

I told myself you were simply lying, that you still loved me dearly.

It was 11 p.m. already, and it was time for me to leave. However, I desperately wanted to stay. After two years of waiting and longing, I couldn't leave like that.

You were a bit startled to hear that I wanted to stay. You didn't say no, adding that you would put a new sheet on the bed for me.

After that, you showed me the other artists' working area, which

I enjoyed in a way. It was quite a huge place with only the two of us there. I felt happy for our luxury of privacy.

Midnight, time to go to bed. I climbed up first, you holding the ladder for me.

I was sitting on your bed waiting for you to come up. As you reached me, you started to cry, with your hands covering your face. You cried out, "I never really thought that you would come to Denmark. It must have been very difficult for you. You…"

I felt your pain, as if it were mine. Our hearts were suffering, tears were falling. I asked you to do something which I always enjoyed, "Can you hug me?"

Yes, you were hugging me with all your love and warmth, embracing me fully, just like before. Everything else was fading away, only love was speaking and listening. And that was what true intimacy meant.

A short loving sentence, "I love you" came to my mind a few times. I wanted so much to say it to you. But I hesitated. We were still crying in each other's arms.

A few minutes later, or maybe a long time later, we stopped crying and decided to go to bed. We were slim, so the small bed fitted us well.

DeDe: "Oskar, you have some small candles here, can we light them up? I like lighting candles very much."

Oskar: "Yes, of course we can."

There we were, lying together on your small bed. You then said with excitement, "Look, from here we can clearly see the stars in the sky!"

I admired your lovely thoughts. I enjoyed watching the stars with you.

A few minutes went by, we were lying in silence, each waiting for the other to initiate something. In the end, you broke the silence by saying, "I don't know why, but I want to kiss you, just like before…"

I felt very happy to hear that.

The Twin Flame Lover of China and Denmark

"Then you should just do it!" I thought in silence, meanwhile, expecting you to kiss me.

You didn't receive my silent message, as we were still lying there. I gently kissed you and quickly turned away. And then you kissed me back. Then we exchanged Love. Love experienced its temporary joy of reunion and the deep pain of the soon-to-follow separation. So many days and nights of love were thus expressed in their own way.

Again, I wished time could stay still, but it didn't. I soon saw the morning light, realizing it was time to face separation again, for the fifth time!

I thought in horror, "I will never see my beloved Oskar again! I don't want to leave! I want to stay! I want to be with my Oskar! But I have to go back because I have my au pair duties to perform. Meanwhile, Oskar is leaving for Mexico the day after tomorrow. Soon, the other artists will arrive and start working. What's the point of staying here any longer? Everything is demanding me to leave! What a destiny!"

Half an hour later, we arrived at the train station. You gave me your train pass and helped me figure out which line I should take.

My heart was bleeding. I had no desire to say anything to you. I was deeply hurt by the words you had said and I felt angry that you never asked me to stay. Speaking rather ironically, I provoked you by saying, "You must feel very happy now, right? Finally, I am leaving. You will never see me again and you are probably feeling very relieved now."

"No. I don't feel happy or relieved. We keep saying goodbye, but we always end up seeing each other again. Maybe we will see each other again..."

What were you really trying to say? I didn't get it. I remained silent, the way I had learned to hold my emotions inside and hide. You did not speak either.

The train arrived and I had to go. For the first time we bid farewell in silence, no eye contact or hugs, for sadness made us feel too fragile to touch each other.

I got on the train, tears falling uncontrollably.

Now, when reflecting on our meeting from a higher state of consciousness, I realize how empty I was inside and how much I was lacking in love back then. I interpreted your every behavior and gesture as a sign of love because I desperately wanted to be loved, instead of being able to give or share love.

I had been wrongly pushing the responsibility of making myself whole and happy onto you, by expecting you to fulfill me. You had sensed my hidden expectations and judgement; feeling trapped or overwhelmed, you continued running even further away. I was unable to give or share love because I had failed to heal myself by looking deep within.

I had been off-track for quite a while. The deep pain and hurt I felt was there to show me how much inner work I needed to do in order to remember who I really am.

It turned out to be a heartbreaking ending because love could never really win out, when there was so much shadow involved. When the heart would understand this, the path of love would unfold and the light would shine through.

A bright new beginning was awaiting me.

Chapter 21

Dark Night of the Soul; Encounter Shela

*I*n despair, I made the decision to go back to Beijing. I concluded that there was no apparent reason for me to stay any longer in Denmark. However, destiny planned otherwise.

I got off the subway and saw Ane waving to me. She lovingly hugged me. I collapsed into her arms, sobbing sadly.

"Ane, I met Oskar yesterday..."

How grateful I was to have dear Ane comforting me, at such a difficult time. A warm hug and an understanding heart was all I needed at that moment. My sadness lessened. Together we walked to Ane's house.

In the afternoon, Ane took me to a forest nearby. She told me that it was once the King of Denmark's hunting forest. There I saw many large, tall trees, pure white snow, and warm sunlight. I enjoyed the fresh clean air there and felt that it was a beautiful place with divine healing energy. I felt good and calm there.

The next morning, I left Ane and Harold's house for my new home.

Mette asked me about my days in Copenhagen. I hesitated, not knowing what to say, and told her that it had been disappointing. I was not ready to tell her the truth but I thought that sooner or later I would do so.

Two days later, on Tuesday, February 12th, after spending nearly three hours cleaning the floor, I was feeling not only physically exhausted but emotionally devastated. It was quite windy and somewhat rainy outside. However, I still rode my bike to the nearby sea.

No one was there. I threw myself to the ground, letting all the concealed pain and hurt come out.

"God, I don't understand all of this! Why did I come to Denmark and why did Oskar say those words to me when I met him in Copenhagen? Why has everything become darker and darker, worse and worse? I have only pain within me now and I don't know what to do about it. Should I just admit that everything which happened is simply a pointless drama? A miserable catastrophe?"

I sobbed for about half an hour. In the end, I decided not to blame anyone any more, including myself. I told myself to stop feeling like a victim. Calmly, I knew it was time for me to take total responsibility for what had happened. The only thing I wanted was to be healed and I desperately wanted to find a healer.

I listened to my intuition, telling me to ride my bike to the town of Ribe, hoping to find a healer there.

"Excuse me, M'am/Sir, do you know if there is a healer living nearby?"

People were helpful, but either they did not know the answer or the healer they knew was living far away. I felt disappointed, but I did not want to give up.

I continued walking and found myself standing outside a shop called, "Den Gamle Butik." I had been to the town a few times before and every time I had passed that shop I always felt special, although I had never gone in.

It was my last hope, so I walked in.

I was immediately enchanted. There were so many lovely unique Danish style vases, teapots, spoons, chocolate, candy, tea, spices, candles and flowers there! Delicate designs, provoking idyllic feelings—what a delightful wonderland!

Meanwhile, I heard a special piece of music playing, music which spoke to my heart and soul. I immersed myself in the music, trying to

The Twin Flame Lover of China and Denmark

understand the meaning of it. The music was not talking about joy or happiness, but pain and sorrow, as if it understood what I had gone through and how I had been feeling. Behind the calmness, it was transmitting messages of letting go and surrendering, suggesting it was the divine solution to the dilemma I was in.

My mind was struggling between the lower and the higher. I wanted to know where the music was from. So I followed the sound and found myself in a special place.

It was a small room with candles burning, with beautiful vases with flowers in them, divine statues and various kinds of spiritual objects. More importantly, I sensed it was a place full of healing energy, uplifting and heart-warming.

I saw wonderful books by the writer Louise Hay, the magical book, *The Secret* by Rhonda Byrne and some other New Age books and DVDs. But what really caught my heart was the inspirational music CDs on the shelf.

I was fascinated by these CDs and I carefully read all the titles. They were called "Fonix Music" and were expressing the energies of joy, peace, calm, power, faith, hope and light. That was exactly what I needed most; it was the kind of music I had been longing so much to listen to! I had now found those invaluable treasures in this spiritual oasis!

A CD titled *The Omen* by Lars Alsing stood out. I thought to myself, "Omen? I learned this word from Paulo Coelho's book, *The Alchemist*. Because of this book and my beloved Oskar, I had come to Denmark. This is a special word for me."

I wanted to buy this CD but at the same time I realized I had totally forgotten my original purpose of asking for a healer. So I walked out of the room.

I saw a nice lady dealing with a few customers in front of her. I guessed she was probably the shop assistant or the owner. After the guests left, I went up to her and asked my question, "Excuse me, M'am, do you know any healer living nearby?"

The Twin Flame Lover of China and Denmark

She looked at me kindly and said, "Yes. I am a healer. May I ask why you are looking for a healer?"

How excited I was! I had finally found my healer!

"I came to Denmark for my beloved but..."

The lady, whose name was Shela, was listening to me attentively. She was not sympathetic to my sorrow or hurt, but her feelings were coming from a compassionate heart. I could feel that her energy was a loving one and on a high level, that she was trustworthy and wise.

I then asked Shela how she had become a healer.

She told me that when she was a small child she could see people's past lives. Those "pictures" were appearing only to her, which made her feel very confused and scared. Her mystical ability was not appreciated by people and she was hurt by some unkind comments from others. It was much later on that she learned how to use her ability properly to help people by offering healing treatments, right in the special small room I had been in.

I realized that clairvoyance was Shela's spiritual gift. In a way, I couldn't believe what I was hearing. But on the other hand, I felt deeply touched and uplifted. What a wonderful blessing to have encountered Shela!

I told Shela I liked her shop very much, especially the lovely music CDs on the shelf. Shela said that I could take the samples of the CDs I liked home to listen to. I felt deeply grateful for her kindness and generosity. I looked forward to listening to those lovely CDs.

After saying goodbye to Shela, I got on my bike and started riding home. My broken heart was feeling warm inside, as if it had been touched by light.

One door had closed earlier, but soon a bright new door had opened.

Chapter 22

Gratitude Changes Surrender

February 16th, 2013, 17:27 pm

I am writing my diary in a lovely café called Quedens in town. I still cannot believe I am now really in Denmark.

I am doing better at housework, but I still need one or two weeks to get it done more efficiently. Language school will probably start this week or next. I am very much looking forward to it. Perhaps I will make one or two good friends there.

For a long time now I have wanted to write down all the blessings I have received along the way:

1. I finally arrived at Denmark. My dream was successfully fulfilled after so much struggling.

2. I have the blessings and love of my family and my good friends.

3. I have Ane and Harold's genuine love and care.

4. The old man working in this café, whom I met on the street today. He asked me, "How are you getting on in Denmark? How's your work? Are you happy in Denmark?" I felt grateful for his warmth and interest, even though I wanted to cry when hearing those questions.

5. One member of staff working in the local church took me up to the top of the steeple, from where I could clearly see the whole of Ribe. Ribe is such a charming fairy tale style town!

6. On February 12th, on my way back from Copenhagen to Bramming, the train I was traveling in broke down; all the passengers had to get off and wait for alternative transport. The Danish

The Twin Flame Lover of China and Denmark

lady who was sitting opposite me very kindly drove me home, which took her one and a half hours. How kind was that!

7. I walked into a local shop named "Dream Arts" the other day. The owner is a nice Danish lady who taught me how to make paper hearts. I received many small sweet paper hearts from her yesterday; I like them a lot.

8. Mette's friend Lone drove me to a nearby dike. There we saw the beautiful ocean frozen in ice. I enjoyed our excursion and felt somewhat happy.

9. Shouldn't I feel grateful that I am provided with a free shower, free water, free food, plus my own nice room in Mette and Thomas's house? That I am staying in such a safe and clean environment, that I also have those free appliances and spices to practice my cooking skills?

10. My Dutch friend Jeroen has prepared a one week travel plan for me. How nice of him! Sometime around June I will visit Holland!

11. My friend Wendy created a very inspiring Wiccan drawing for me! How special!

12. The sun in Denmark is much bigger than it is in Beijing. The beautiful sunlight from the sky shining upon the fields and the ocean is so amazing! It made me feel that I am so close to the divine Creator, that She/He is generous and loving, full of power and light!

13. In the evening, from the window of my room, I can clearly see the sky filled with millions of shining stars! It is my time to dream, use my imagination, to dance and experience love!

14. I met the magical healer Shela!

What has been happening to me feels strange and unbelievable. Looking back, so many changes have taken place! This strange process makes me feel awestruck. I am neither happy nor miserable. I feel I am in a process of learning and waiting for things to unfold at their right time, as Destiny decrees.

Remember: you are the master of your destiny, the captain of your soul.

Writing this diary was positive and uplifting. Soon afterwards I re-established my ritual of meditating and dancing daily, which had a positive influence on me.

On February 19th, I went to the city of Esbjerg for my English test, the result of which would determine my level as a beginner learning Danish. As Mette had foreseen, my level was the highest—level three. I felt good about that.

I was told I had two choices regarding my Danish classes. The first one was that I could go to school three times a week every Monday, Wednesday and Thursday, from 8 a.m. to 2 p.m. The second was for me to attend school only twice a week every Monday and Wednesday, from 6 p.m. to 8 p.m.

Learning Danish had never been my primary intention and I regarded it as a rather difficult language; therefore, I took the second option.

My first class was arranged for the following Wednesday and I was looking forward to it.

Before attending school, I made three positive changes:

1. Get up early in the morning and finish doing my housework by 11 a.m.

2. Spend my time and money wisely.

3. Go to the local library in town regularly and get myself into the habit of reading and writing.

I decided on these changes because I realized there was something wrong with just sitting there, doing nothing but merely wishing a great master would appear and teach me. It was time to shape my reality by myself! Who could decide and influence the future? Only the spirit and the energy flowing inside of me.

In the evening of February 27th I went to the language school in town and attended my first Danish class.

Other students in the class had been learning Danish for a few months already, so they could understand and speak some Danish, whereas I was the only one who didn't know any Danish at all.

The Twin Flame Lover of China and Denmark

During the whole class, I felt rather discouraged. Deeply confused, I asked myself what was the point of learning Danish and why should I bother.

Another hurricane had come into my life. Triggered by this new development, I became rebellious about everything and I slid backwards down the slope of progress. More seriously, I decided to go back to Beijing.

I confessed to Mette and Thomas about my real purpose for coming to Denmark and about my intention to leave. They had enough reasons to be angry with me. However, they were generous and forgiving people. After hearing the hard truth, they still wished for me to stay and even said that I was free to choose to stay for six months or one year instead of the two years we had originally agreed to.

I was deeply grateful for their kindness and I asked them to give me one week to think it through.

"Do I fight because I already see hope or because I want to create hope?" I asked myself this question. Realizing it was an important decision which would alter the course of my life, I asked God to help me make the right decision.

On March 9th I told Mette and Thomas that I had decided to stay for one year. They were happy to hear that. Mette even said that it was a good decision, which deserved a celebration. I felt a bit embarrassed, but quite warm inside; I also felt relieved at having made this decision.

I told myself to be patient and surrender to the life I had chosen; I reminded myself to have faith in my future and remember the infinite power of my mind. Meanwhile, I switched from my evening language class to the intensive day class. Because I had made the decision to learn Danish, even though I had no particular reason to do so, I was determined to make my Danish outstanding within a few months.

As for Oskar, I blessed him for the choice he had made, telling myself not to think about him any more. I put all my trust in God, believing She/He would reveal the truth in the end and bring ultimate happiness to us all.

I wrote in my diary:

Maybe it's time to forget.

The truth is: Oskar doesn't love you any more.

You move on with peace and hope.

You throw away all the hurt and disappointment to the wind.

And you look forward to the beautiful springtime of your soul.

By this time, my routine was basically formed: "Get up at around 6:30 a.m. and finish morning cleaning duties by 7:30 a.m.; ride my bike to school and attend class at 8 a.m.; after school, at 2 p.m., go to the library and read there for one or two hours; around 5 p.m. or so, ride back home, etc."

On the two non-school days, I would also ride my bike to the library to read or simply have a walk in town after finishing my cleaning duties by 11 a.m.

Life was becoming fixed between home, school and library. A life like that felt simple and repetitive. However, at the same time, life had become meaningful and enjoyable. All because I started to dance!

Early in February I wrote emails to my friend Wendy, in which I complained about the boredom of doing housework. Wendy suggested asking Mette if they had a CD player so that she could mail me some CDs to listen to while doing housework. I listened to her suggestion and asked Thomas about a CD player.

On February 12th, after I came home from Shela's shop, I saw a nice CD player standing right in front of my door. How surprised and joyful I was! How kind of Thomas to give it to me!

I listened to the CDs I brought from Shela's shop and I liked them a lot. I wanted to buy many more of them, but the total cost was too much for me.

A few days later I went to the local library for the first time. The kind librarian recognized that I was a new face and said to me, "You

The Twin Flame Lover of China and Denmark

know, you are welcome to come here to read or to borrow any books or CDs. If the books or CDs you want are not in this library, we will phone other libraries in Denmark and order them for you, you just need to wait a few days. This is totally free for you because you have a resident permit card."

I was so impressed by such a wonderful service offered in Denmark. I felt very excited to hear what she had said and I immediately inquired if they could order some Fonix Music CDs for me.

Yes, they could—exactly the same CDs that I had seen in Shela's shop. What a blessing!

At the beginning I was listening only to these CDs and I was practicing my dancing ritual which I had created in Beijing. However, I later on was guided to dance to the music.

Since the middle of March, after finishing my evening cleaning routine around 7:30 p.m., I would always go to my room, turn the music on and start to dance, immersing myself into the beautiful energies of the music, embracing my deepest feelings and emotions, reaching for my deepest inner self and freely dancing with my soul.

I heard the divine messages transmitting to me: "Redeem the past, surrender to the now, believe in the future, trust yourself, transcend your personality, transform your life, be strong, keep dancing...the beautiful time is coming..."

Almost every night, I would dance from 7:30 p.m. to 9:30 p.m. A magical transforming journey started right from there, guided by the divine soul dancer living within me.

Music and dance have the power to transform our world, especially when they are combined with healing energy. What kind of mystical ability could become activated? What wonderful potential of mine could be awakened?

I didn't know the answer to these question, but I simply felt better and better, lighter and lighter, as if I was being healed, uplifted and transformed by an invisible powerful Higher Energy.

Mette even praised me: "DeDe, you are really doing better and better! Seems like there is a flowing rhythm in what you are doing!"

I felt happy to hear that and I replied, "Thank You, Mette! It's because I dance almost every day now! My dance makes me feel alive and flowing!"

Chapter 23

The First Healing Session With Shela

As arranged on March 20th, on a Wednesday at 6 p.m., I arrived at Shela's shop for my first healing treatment. Shela's hug was warm and loving and made me feel very good. I loved her elegant clothes. The beautiful necklace she was wearing caught my heart and soul. The design of it, the light of it, and the healing energy of it made me feel in awe. I secretly wished I could have one like that as well.

We walked into the healing room together. I saw one small bed with pretty blankets on it; right beside the bed there was a small round desk with a vase and a special bronze bowl on it. Inside the vase, there was a beautiful flower.

I felt happy and special to be there. The room was full of spiritual healing energy. I couldn't wait to discover what would happen next.

Shela asked me what I would like to know. I told her I wanted to know something about my true love and why I had come to Denmark.

Shela asked me to lie down on the healing bed and covered me with a soft blanket. She asked me to close my eyes and take few deep breaths. I did as she instructed, enjoying the warmth and comfort, at the same time waiting, full of curiosity about what would happen next.

My eyes were closed, but my heart and my ears were not. With heightened sensitivity and with excitement I was sensing what was happening every single second. I heard Shela take a few deep breaths and walk somewhere close to me. She then said something strange. I assumed it was a holy invocation.

Shela then sat on a chair close to me. I heard her turn on the music; it was *Rainbow Theme* by the New Age musician Frank Lorentzen. I started to feel even more special and more curious.

I heard Shela continue breathing deeply to adjust to something, or rather, to invoke something. A few minutes later, I heard her start to write something in a notebook. And then, the invocation and the writing continued. I wondered what Shela was doing exactly and if she was receiving some information about me from some mystical channel.

About 20 minutes later, she stopped writing and walked somewhere close to me. Again I was aware of her deep breathing and another invocation. And then, all of a sudden, I heard a very strange sound, as if a kind of explosion had occurred. Or rather, a mystical exchange. As if a mystical high being had descended from heaven and just walked into Shela!

Yes, that is what it was. I then heard a voice saying something strange. No, that voice was not Shela's. It was the voice of the mystical high being! It sounded ancient, slow and distant. As if it was not easy or common for the mystical being to speak in the world of humans, as if lots of frequency adjustments needed to be made. The language spoken was neither English nor Danish and sounded rather strange. I called it Star Language.

I felt nervous and excited. I told myself to relax and put my total trust in Shela.

Then, Shela, or rather, the mystical being, put her hands at the bottom of my feet for about three minutes. Her hands felt extremely warm. After that, she felt the areas above my belly, heart, throat, and brain. I was aware she was checking my chakras.

I then heard another strange sound, as if the mystical being had walked out of Shela. Yes, that was it exactly. Shela's voice had become what it was like before. She gently said that I could open my eyes.

Shela was sitting right next to me, with the notebook in her hands. She said to me, "DeDe, you are a big person, not a small person. Your energy is very strong and powerful. Your heart pattern is the most beautiful one I have ever seen. But there are some people and certain things which are stuck in there; they are preventing your heart from feeling the kind of happiness or emotions it wants to feel. You need to work on resolving these obstacles, clearing the path and opening your heart.

"Your connection with the Higher Energy is very strong. You are a creative and imaginative person. You are very good at using the Higher Energy to create the kind of reality you want–that is your inborn gift and uniqueness.

"Since your connection with Heavenly Energy is so strong, therefore, life on Earth can make you feel anxious and confused. You very much want to live in your center, but you find it to be difficult. You are lacking in Earth Energy. Trees have appeared many times in your dreams because they want to help you. If you hug them and absorb their energy, it will be very good for you. Try to find your way to balance your Heavenly Energy with your Earth Energy.

"Colors are important to you and you like them very much. One day, you will use them. Your hands are not particularly sensitive yet, you don't like doing handicraft activities, but your hands are very important to you.

"I saw someone who is waiting for you in the future. Since your energy is so strong and powerful, your other half must also possess the same level of energy as you do. You do not have any real soul level friends yet; they too are waiting for you in the future.

"Your time in Denmark will be a very important time for you. You came here in order to find out who you really are and who you want to be. Only after you find out who you are and become your true self, will your other half and your true friends appear in your life."

What Shela said about me was totally true. I was simply amazed.

I wondered who was waiting for me in the future. I found it to be rather challenging to hear that my other half and true friends would appear only after I became who I was born to be. I saw this to be quite a huge test and I doubted if I had the strength and wisdom to successfully come through it some day.

I then talked with Shela for a while regarding something else. Soon my one and a half hour healing session was up and it was time for me to go home and for Shela to pick up her daughter.

We said goodbye to each other. With love and a feeling of warmth, I left her shop and rode my bike back home.

Chapter 24

Changes From April to August

*E*aster holidays started on March 23rd. I took the train to Copenhagen and stayed at Ane and Harold's house for six nights. They took good care of me and I enjoyed visiting some lovely scenic spots in Copenhagen. So many times I couldn't help laughing with joy because the dream, which I once considered "impossible," was being realized. Upon leaving, somewhere in my heart I deeply wished that I could visit this charming city again with a higher new identity.

On April first I took the train back. Thomas picked me up from the train station. On the way, I said to him, "Thomas, I quite enjoyed the trip to Copenhagen. But actually, I've been missing my life here quite a lot."

There I was, back to my small village Farup and to my established routine of doing housework, reading and writing, dancing and meditating. My journey of evolution continued.

I was very impressed about the fact that the sun now started to set around 8:30 p.m. Mette told me that as time went on the sun would set as late as 11 p.m. That was something I had never experienced and I felt this to be quite interesting. I didn't enjoy dancing in my room while it was still light outside, so from around the middle of April I would always ride my bike to the nearby forest to dance for two hours. I thoroughly enjoyed my new dancing routine.

Dance and meditation continued to transform me. I started to seriously think about what my life's work should be and how I could serve humanity through my interests and likes; my new self image had become clearer to me and I started to firmly believe that to live a life with joy, financial security, meaning and beauty was possible. My attitude toward time had changed; I felt it moving faster and realized its vital importance. As a result of this discovery, I decided to arrange my time more constructively and meaningfully.

Life is always in constantly changing motion and when you decide to evolve and become a better person, life will in turn respond to you on a higher frequency.

Call it coincidence or destiny—I met my Danish friend Benny on the train journey during my Easter holiday. I then met another Danish friend Ole in the local library; what's more, I met Chi at my language school and we soon became good friends. She was from Vietnam and was also working as an au pair with a local Danish family, so we had lots to share and talk about.

My dear friends Benny, Ole and Chi had brought much love and joy into my life; they warmed my days, just like the sunshine. I felt deeply grateful for their company.

During the whole month of May, the main theme of my thoughts was about finding ways to justify my life. This is what I wrote in my diary:

"I desperately want to justify my life and my existence. It's about having the courage to dare to think what kind of life you truly want and deserve; and then, having the courage to believe it is possible and backing this up with actions to fulfill it. For me, it means to have the patience and faith to believe that soon I will figure out what my life work is!

"When life was given, it was meant to be beautiful, materially secure and loving. There are many people in this world who have successfully achieved such a life; I choose to become one of them.

"From now on, I need to train my mind to think more positively and think more frequently about the life I truly deserve and desire! Higher new thoughts and visions must be created in order to match who I am becoming.

"Without Oskar, my family or the Double Happiness Courtyard Hotel, when I am here alone almost every day, my main focus has turned to myself, especially my career and my inner world. A new self image has been created in my mind: 'She is centered, grounded, financially secure, strong and wise; she is loving to herself and others; shining inside and outside.'

"This is the self I want to become and I know I am becoming her. One day, I will fully be her and be illuminated by her special light.

"Dear Spirits, please continue guiding me, as I walk toward the wonderful vision you have for me; let me keep dancing and meditating so that I will continue building up the power to transform and evolve; help me allow and welcome all the good things I deserve in life; teach me to have the willingness and patience to wait for the right time to carry out my mission.

"Life is a divine gift and we ought to treat it as such. It is time to learn how to focus our energy on creating a beautiful life; time to think and act differently, with courage and honor!"

By the end of May, I had the feeling that a stage of my development had finished—a stage within which I had established my personal routine and ritual. Deep down, I hoped that something higher would unfold as time went on. In other words, I deeply longed for more growth and higher revelations.

Invited by my Dutch friend Jeroen, I visited Holland for nine days, traveling on June 1st. Jeroen was a friend whom I had met at the Double Happiness Courtyard hotel in 2011 and who had generously offered me much support along my journey. He and his family took good care of me and made my Holland trip memorable and enjoyable. I felt grateful for everything that was so kindly offered during that trip.

I came back to Denmark with a fresh new attitude toward my life and, most importantly, I decided to learn Danish with my whole heart and soul. My Danish friend Ole volunteered to become my

The Twin Flame Lover of China and Denmark

private Danish teacher and we met twice a week at the local library to practice Danish. With his help and my dedication, my Danish progressed considerably and I started to enjoy the wonder of speaking a new language with people.

I told myself, "Listen to the silence, dance with the hidden rhythm and concentrate on the inner fire; trust that the invisible golden hand will finally guide you to where you are meant to be."

As the dancing and the cleaning activities were going on, I had the sensation that my mind and body were being aligned and healed. I carefully checked through all my stuff and threw away many things that I did not feel connected to any more. I wanted to have a different hair style and I felt my clothes did not suit me any more. I redefined my perception of beauty by incorporating elegance and grace. I realized I could simplify my life just as much as I could purify my thoughts. I realized I had created everything that had happened in my life and that I was in charge of my destiny.

Later on, reading from Sanaya Roman's wonderful book *Spiritual Growth–Being Your Higher Self*, I realized I was going through the void by letting go of the old and moving to my new level of growth; I was raising my vibration and expanding my vision. It was an important time of transition and change.

Change continued unfolding; by the beginning of July, a more definite and clearer New Self had emerged.

"She is beautiful, loving, shining and soft, a reflection of her inner gentleness and loving; she is financially secure, capable, and confident; she is walking her path and she knows the charming secrets of another world; she has become at one with her soul and she is emitting the light of love and wisdom; she remembers and activates her true identity–The Divine Beautiful Goddess."

I asked myself when and how I could finally become the Goddess. The answer came to me: "Follow and honor the spirit; most importantly, keep dancing."

Time flew by so quickly; the summer holidays had arrived. By then, my friend Chi had already moved to her new host family who lived in the second biggest city of Denmark—Arhus. The family had gone away for their holiday and Chi would be free to have her own holiday when they came back. So in the middle of July I took the train to Arhus and planned to stay with Chi for a week.

We went around the town, walking, biking, sightseeing, and shopping; we spent our time cooking, talking and just hanging out. We shared a lot of excitement and joy. I admired her talent for cooking and decorating, whereas she admired my gift of speaking and expressing myself. We also frankly exchanged our deep inner concerns about the unknown future lying ahead of us. When we parted, we encouraged each other to continue our search; we both believed that as long as we didn't give up, one day, God would reward us with the wonderful gifts we sought after.

One week later, I took the train back home. After arriving at the train station, I needed to take a bus. I embarked and was quite surprised to discover that I was the only passenger on the bus.

I took my bus fare—20 Danish Kroner from my wallet and handed it to the bus driver. However, I was astonished when he said, "Aha! Today it is free for you; you don't need to pay anything."

I said to him: "Wow, you are so nice and kind. But excuse me, may I ask why?"

"Because today we are having such nice weather. We need to celebrate it! So, it is free for you!"

I felt happy to hear that and really admired his joyful spirit. We then started to chat regarding the weather, the food and the language, etc.

About ten minutes later, before I got off the bus, I offered him some fresh cherries which I had picked up in Arhus. He thanked me for my kindness and I certainly appreciated his.

Mette and Thomas were still on holiday. I arrived at home and felt a bit alone. However, I couldn't wait to ride my bike to the forest to dance with the spirit.

The Twin Flame Lover of China and Denmark

In August, another bigger wave of change followed; my yearning for a better and more fulfilling life had become stronger. I was determined to break all previous limitations I had set for myself and I realized it was time to free my mind and allow many higher new possibilities to flow into my life.

I recalled how, when I was little, my parents had to leave me and my sister at home to work in a factory in Guangzhou, where the conditions were harsh. They worked so hard and saved every penny of their meagre income, so that I could go to school. A few years later, they came back home and started to grow rice, as they had done before. They suffered a lot to pay for my tuition so that I could attend high school and graduate from college.

I asked myself, "Have I really appreciated my ability to speak English? And more importantly, have I used it fully to make enough money to justify my life and thank my parents?"

The answer was no. I realized that I had taken something important for granted; it was time to truly value myself and my talents; time to think and act in higher ways; time to ascend from the little self to the Higher Self!

Chapter 25

Second Healing Session With Shela

At the beginning of September, Mette and Thomas asked me when I would like to go home because it would be better to book my flight ticket three months beforehand. I told them I would prefer to go at the beginning of December.

By this time, I already had a positive understanding about the whole picture. I saw clearly that my meeting with Oskar was meant to be; I realized that the underlying reason why I had traveled all the way to Denmark was to awaken my Higher Self by dancing, meditating and going through the void. Everything that had happened made sense to me, and I acknowledged that it was all for my spiritual growth and higher good.

However, somewhere deep in my heart I was feeling unsatisfied and unfulfilled, especially when I still didn't know what I would like to do after going back. I looked for something extraordinary to happen. Or rather, I wished something matching to my soul's deepest longing and searching could appear to reward my journey.

Around the middle of September, I suddenly had an inspiration. I thought about going back to Beijing and finding a new job; then, most importantly, I thought of using my free time to turn my story into a book. I figured that my story might help and uplift people by my example of following my dreams and transforming my life. I felt very excited and joyful when I began to imagine myself as one of the most inspiring New Age writers in the world. In all seriousness, I asked myself, "Since I like reading and writing so much, does it mean that my calling is to become a writer?"

I didn't think any further about it because I had doubts about myself and my writing ability. However, in my heart I still felt quite joyful when I thought about this new inspiration!

After that, I agreed with Mette and Thomas on my preferred leaving date. They booked my plane ticket for December 7th. On the one hand, I felt relieved and relaxed. On the other hand, I wondered if it was indeed the right choice. In fact, I had been thinking about it for some weeks. In order to see things more clearly, in early September I booked another healing session with Shela which was to take place on September 19th.

That day at 8:30 a.m. I arrived at Shela's shop. I felt the same excitement as on the previous occasion, but this time I was a totally different self.

The procedure was more or less the same, except that Shela, having sensed my chakras, asked me to imagine this: "It is very early in the morning, everything is fresh and active. You are walking in a beautiful forest, you can see and smell the grass, you are feeling happy and good. Then, on your right hand side you see a small road and you walk along it.

"Now you see a house. You walk into the house and see an elevator. There are five floors. You look at number one—no, that's not where you want to go; you look at number two—no, again, that's not where you want to go either. Then you see number three, you press the button and you arrive at the third floor. There, you see a beautiful room and you walk in. There are people in this room. And now, you need to ask the people there any questions you want to ask."

Shela left me alone and walked out of the room.

I imagined the scenario, as she had instructed. My house was a kind of white colored building, not as beautiful or lovely as I would have liked it to be, but simple and clean. My room was also simple and clean, with flowers in it. There, I saw a very wise, gentle and loving white-haired old lady. She was wearing pure white, elegant clothes, and she had a divinely peaceful aura around her. She even had two or more spiritual guides standing behind her. She seemed caring and it seemed as if she had been waiting there for me for a while.

I was not sure afterwards if I had asked her any questions or whether she had answered them, because after all, everything was happening in an imagined world. But I did remember clearly, that when we were silently conversing, she had a white envelope in her hands. And before we parted, she handed it to me.

Now came the craziest part. After returning from my imagined world, Shela came in and asked what I had seen. I told her everything. Right after I mentioned the white envelope I had seen, Shela gave me a white envelope! It was almost the same as I had seen in my imagination! At that moment, both of us felt very awestruck.

Shela told me that while I was imagining the encounter with the old lady, she was writing something on a card and that she had then put it in that white envelope.

Coincidence or what? Things were becoming strange and I wanted so much to know what Shela had seen and written.

The words written on the card were all in Danish; I found it difficult to fully understand their meaning, so Shela explained to me the following: "DeDe, your body, mind and spirit are now in an almost completely harmonious state. That must be the result of your hard work. Last time, they were totally broken and distorted.

Your third eye has been awakening. One day, you will use it to see things and help people.

"Your heart chakra is starting to open, but in order to let it fully awaken and to develop yourself more, you will need the energies of mountains to help you. I see some places for you, perhaps the northern part of England, Scotland, Finland or Norway.

"You are not ready to go home yet. You still need some time to fully develop yourself. If you go back to Beijing and start living a normal life, it will be very difficult for you to finish the journey you have already started."

I felt very happy to hear Shela's statements about my progress. However, at the same time I felt extremely confused and unsettled about the suggestion of going to another country after my time in Denmark. I did not want to do it, because I felt it would be rather difficult and exhausting, especially after experiencing several rather difficult months in Denmark already.

For the next two weeks I struggled a lot when considering where exactly I should go. In the end, because of the visa situation, I listened to my inner voice, which was telling me that I should go back to Beijing, with the understanding that Shela might be right and that I could follow her suggestion at some later point in time.

I wrote in my diary: "Always listen to the heart. Always remember the power to choose. Choose what kind of thoughts to think about your unknown future. Make sure those thoughts are full of confidence and love, as well as financial security.

"I am aware of myself. I am winning and I am already a winner because I have got rid of any bad habits and have cultivated many meaningful ones; I have conquered myself and I am reaching for my highest self. I must trust the ending of my journey will be great and wonderful; an end full of love and light!"

Chapter 26

Important Changes and the Discovery of the Twin Flame

October 1st, 2013, 14:54 p.m., at the library
What does it mean to love and honor yourself, and to honor what you do?

One day recently, while I was doing some cleaning, I again felt quite bored. Suddenly I thought, "It seems that I have had a very clear idea about what is meaningful and what is meaningless." Because all along I had been judging housework to be meaningless and pointless!

But can I actually tell what is meaningful and what is not? Have I learned how to appreciate myself and what I do? Especially as an au pair performing her cleaning jobs? How do I feel about being an au pair? Do I think it is an insult to who I am? Or do I choose to think and perceive its importance as being the same as being the president of the United States? If there were no cleaning ladies in the world, then, could any home be called a real home? Could any country be a clean country?

And then, how do I perceive other people's jobs? What about a gardener, a farmer, a teacher, and what about people who made the clothes and shoes I am wearing right now? What about the cups I've been using to drink water every day, bikes I've been riding between home and school, books and pens I've been enjoying using for reading and writing? Right now, at this very moment, the pen I am writing with, the notebook I am writing in, the chair, the table, this library, this library's windows, the music CDs I've been listening to...

According to my previous silly standards of what I considered to be meaningful and meaningless, all the people who have participated in creating the above-mentioned items are all useless and their jobs are all meaningless, just like my au pair work.

It's time to shift my perceptions to a deeper level, time to appreciate everything that has been kindly offered to me, time to realize that everyone's contribution is equally important. Builders, musicians, teachers, cleaners, etc.–they are all spiritual in a way. Everyone needs everyone; we all need each other's contributions; and we are all connected!

No matter what kind of illusions or masks people are wearing, I should choose to use my soul's eyes to see the deepest core of their being; I should love and join them.

Imagine: if this world only had people like me who like writing, dancing and meditating, how boring it would be! God gave different people different talents, likes and interests. I can't just distance myself from or not love them because they don't do or believe what I do and believe.

Imagine: no matter where I am and what I do, if I choose to love and honor myself, love and accept people the way they are, honor what they do, and then we exchange love from our hearts, how loving and rich our life will then be!

Birth and death, one life after another, circle and another circle–we are all on the road to reach final enlightenment; we all are trying our very best to grow and evolve. Therefore, it is important to remember to love and honor the self, as well as others.

This is perhaps a huge shift that happened to my thinking pattern last night, a profound improvement of the mind.

Dear spirits, may you guide me, always.

October 5th, 2013, 10:38 a.m., at the library
I also recently discovered another mistake in my old thinking patterns: I used to think things were fixed and that once I arrived

at a certain level, for example, in my English skills, my spiritual development, or my relationships with other people, that I would remain at that level, because if I were to change, things might get worse and I might lose what I already had achieved.

I had been thinking in that silly way before and I expected others to act and think the same way as I did. Now, I realize that by thinking and acting like that, I had stopped myself from growing and learning!

The truth is, you should always be constantly learning new things and skills, gaining new inspirations and revelations, expanding and evolving. Just like in nature, everything in this universe is always in a changing motion, and we need to listen to our inner voice in order to achieve the highest level of change.

One important question: how can people become their best selves and how can they realize their dreams?

This morning I called my father, after talking about this and that, I asked him a question, "Dad, what was your dream when you were young?"

He replied, "Dreams? I had many dreams in my youth. I dreamed of being a great calligrapher, a very good singer and an excellent speaker. But life..."

My father has a great talent for calligraphy. He writes very beautifully, inspired by his spirit and soul. When he was only seven or eight years old, his writing was as good as his teacher's.

My mother wanted to be a wonderful tailor. She is very good at making clothes. When my sister and I were young, she enjoyed making lots of beautiful and colorful clothes for us.

My mother and father sacrificed themselves for me and my sister. They became poorly paid factory workers and then hard working farmers, all because they wanted to provide for me and my sister a better life with more choices. I am the only girl in our village who went to college. Because of it, I had the great opportunity to improve my English, to come to Beijing and Denmark and then to become who I am today.

And now, it is my turn to make some important choices. I am sure my interests are writing, healing, dancing and spiritual counseling. But a more specific vision and further details have not emerged yet. In order to fulfill all my dreams and be successful, I need to strengthen my spirit and keep walking on the right track.

I am dedicated to the belief that one day I will be all I was born to be. I will be super successful and super happy. I am the cheer-up master of my own life!

October 13th, 2013, 08:40 a.m., in my bedroom
Because of our lack of awareness, childhood programming and false beliefs about who we are and what we deserve, we may experience much pain and hurt as we grow up. Sometimes our life seems to fall into a painful dark hole.

We unconsciously attract these experiences and people to ourselves and they in turn teach us the most important life lessons we need to learn. That is why we need to forgive ourselves and others.

With compassion and wisdom, we need to take total responsibility for cleaning up the mess we had created and healing ourselves. I know now that we all have the power to heal ourselves through dance, meditation, reflection and by asking for divine guidance. When we ask, we receive. It is all a matter of faith and belief.

I know so clearly now that it is most important to love and accept myself more and more, to put my life into a higher and more organized order, to create a future full of joy, love, support, meaning and happiness.

(End of Diaries)

Ever since I knew I would be going back to Beijing in December, there was a deep wish in my heart, a longing for something extraordinary to happen before leaving Denmark. What exactly was it that I longed for so desperately? Only my soul knew. Somehow, destiny decided it was time to lift the veil and reveal the puzzle.

The Twin Flame Lover of China and Denmark

One day during the second half of October I went to the local library as usual, aiming to use the computer there to watch some inspiring music videos from the New Age musician Medwyn Goodall, whose music had been influencing and inspiring my dance routines.

For the first time in my life I opened YouTube. After a while I was somehow guided to a page full of videos about the Twin Flame. The moment I saw these two words I felt a very strange sensation and I wondered, "Twin Flame? What does this mean? I understand the meaning of 'twin' and 'flame' but when the two words are together as a concept, it doesn't mean anything to me at all."

I wasn't sure if I wanted to watch these videos, but then, a sudden impulse coming from seemingly nowhere made me really curious. I had an urge to know something about it. So I opened the first video, explaining the Twin Flame concept. The second video explained the important signs indicating this kind of relationship, then others detailed the various stages of such a relationship–the runner and the chaser dynamic... etc.

I am truly grateful to the Twin Flame writers and to those who posted these videos, because suddenly I understood everything. Oskar is the other half of my soul–my Twin Flame! I knew he was someone very special right at the beginning!

All the clouds were lifted by the wise words and I was blessed enough to see the ultimate truth!

I had decided to go back to Beijing in the belief that what had happened between me and Oskar was merely a drama. But when I was about to give up, this significant revelation was shown to me. Can you imagine how happy and excited I was?

On the way back home that day, I definitely experienced a mystical, beautiful sensation, as if my soul was singing and dancing in pure joy and light. I recalled Paulo Coelho's quote, "Some day everything will make perfect sense. So, for now, laugh at the confusion, smile through the tears and keep reminding yourself that everything happens for a reason."

The Twin Flame Lover of China and Denmark

October 24th, 2013, evening, in my bedroom

Recent days have been quite overwhelming to me, especially my discovery about the Twin Flames. Today I was inspired to research more information about Twin Flame relationships on the Internet and, to my great surprise, many people are talking and writing about this concept. After reading some inspiring writings I gained a better understanding about what it all means. For example, someone has written, "It is only when the chaser gets completely rejected by the runner, that she will begin walking her path of enlightenment."

Also, last night my mind suddenly became very creative and finally, I came to understand how to blend my interests and the activity I enjoy doing most, which is writing! By reading great and inspiring books I absorb great wisdom and accumulate lots of high level information. Through writing I can then deliver the highest truths to others and cause important changes to occur in their lives!

To be a spiritual, thoughtful, inspiring and influential writer! To ask important questions and have deep meaningful conversations with people! To travel and write about wonderful experiences! To lead and encourage my readers to think and act to fulfill their dreams! And, at the same time, to create meaning and material security for my life!

Does it sound like another impossible dream or is it too beautiful to become a reality?

I think I am willing to challenge myself. Life is a succession of thoughts and I believe that to realize my writer's dream is possible!

For my parents, as farmers, their job is to grow rice and corn; for my uncle, as a carpenter, his enjoyment comes from making beautiful chairs and tables; my friend Chi dreams of being a wonderful cook. For me, as a writer, my job is to think greater and higher thoughts, to encourage, uplift, inspire and transform! To lead people to free their minds by shattering their limited consciousness so that they can fully embrace the truth of love and life and live a fulfilling and happy life.

The Twin Flame Lover of China and Denmark

If I had not come to Denmark I would never have logged onto YouTube and got to know about the Twin Flames; I would never have understood what has been really happening between us.

During my period of great pain and confusion, I had asked for a great master to teach and heal me. After these few months I have discovered that the Great Master actually resides within me! It is my Higher Self! She has been educating me all along the way! Thank You!

It seems that today is the day when everything is coming together from different places, in the way I have always hoped for. I have found my treasures! Thank you, dear spirits!

Chapter 27

Drum Dance and Spiritual Awakening

There are many sacred ways to reach enlightenment. Some achieve it through meditation, using a mantra, practicing yoga, adopting breathing techniques, etc. Each person's approach is different, yet all paths lead to the same goal. In my case, dancing has served as the divine doorway for me to enter into a higher state of consciousness and has offered me much healing and growth. I feel it is my joyful responsibility to write about it in more details before I finish writing about my experiences in Denmark. I therefore invite you to dance in your creative imagination as you continue reading this chapter.

During the early stage of my dancing, from the middle of March until May, I would listen to some relaxing music by the artists Bindu, Egil Fylling, Frantz Amathy, Mike Rowland, and Jan Skovgaard Peter to serve as accompaniment to my dance. As a result, my body movements were soft and slow.

However, one day, while I was listening to the CD, *The Omen* by artist Lars Alsing, I was suddenly attracted to its drum beats. I felt as if those drum beats were calling and awakening me. From the moment I was introduced to this CD I discovered it was by the Danish artist Steen Raahauge who had composed the music. I felt very happy about my discovery and consequently I borrowed many of Steen Raahauge's CDs from the library. Since then, most of the time I've been dancing to his music.

Mystical, ancient, powerful, strong, awakening, exploring,

inspiring... are the words that best describe Steen Raahauge's music. When I was listening to his music I felt as if I was brought to an ancient mystical primitive tribe where people were at one with the heaven, the Earth, the divine, the drum, the dance, the strength, and the soul of the universe. The beats, the rhythm and the energy contained therein are full of strength and power. Within the music there are no moments for you to feel weak or small, but it constantly inspires and drives you to move on and wake up, wake up to your deep buried truth and higher potential.

It was as if it was saying to me, "So, come and join us. You are meant to be a dancer! You were made to be powerful and full of energy! Come and dance!"

Right! Come and dance! Follow your heart and surrender to the divine calling of your soul. Do not think about being perfect or developing any technical skills; know that the highest form of any dance is to dance with the soul.

Most days from May to September I had been dancing in the forest from 8 p.m. to 10 p.m. with bare feet. No other people were there, only the surrounding big green trees and the deep blue sky above. I felt deeply blessed to be able to dance in such a divinely beautiful forest.

I applied all my strength and attention to be able to dance, to move, to jump, to move to the beat and to awaken myself. So many times I thought to myself, "I really don't know why I am using my whole being to dance like this. I only know this is my calling now, the only activity which enhances my life and gives me energy. Nothing that has happened makes any sense to me, but through my dancing I try to justify it all. I must dance all my sadness and pain away! I must rise up by regaining my strength and power! I declare this is the rebirth of my soul!"

Yes, every single cell was evolving and transforming. I was going through a mystical process of healing and transcending. Day after day, night after night, slowly, slowly, I no longer felt small or hurt; I became transformed. I felt strong and centered. Looking at myself in the mirror I noticed my eyes were shining with hope and joy. I smiled at myself, feeling delighted to see my new self embracing the light.

I also noticed that some time between August and November, unusual changes were happening to me:

1. My hands and my feet became very warm, as if there was electricity flowing inside them. Almost my entire body felt that way as well, especially during August and September.

2. For many days, I had a problem with diarrhea.

3. So many nights I would naturally wake up around 2 or 4 a.m. and then fall sound asleep again.

4. Suddenly, at the beginning of August my third eye started to awaken and from then on I experienced its opening.

5. Suddenly, I often started to feel hungry.

6. Some time during late October I just couldn't tolerate eating meat any more because I felt as if I and the animals were one. To see their meat being cut or simply washed made me want to vomit. It had become something too cruel for me to witness. Very suddenly and very naturally, I had become a vegetarian and I felt very, very happy about it. Somewhere deep in my heart I wondered what all these experiences signified.

By November, I had already finished my Danish classes at school. As a result, every day after finishing my cleaning duties I found myself having a lot of free time. In order to figure out all that had happened I kept going to the library and researching everything I wanted to know about.

I typed into the search engine such words and phrases as spiritual awakening, kundalini, Twin Flame, enlightenment, ascension symptoms, light worker, light body, star seeds, dimension. After much reading and deliberating, a bigger picture had emerged.

"I am a light worker, as is my beloved Oskar. Our mission is to bring light to the world through our service, just like many other

The Twin Flame Lover of China and Denmark

light workers."

In a true Twin Flame relationship, spiritual awakening stages go hand in hand with relationship stages. Each stage of our relationship marked a new stage of my spiritual development. From 2009 until the present, I had been experiencing a spiritual awakening. These strange changes that happened to me were signs of a spiritual awakening!

I thought I had come to Denmark solely for Oskar but no, I was sent here for many bigger and deeper reasons.

"I now see clearly why I came to Denmark! I came here to arise from my little self to the higher self by living in the void in this small and quiet village; to expand, heal and evolve; to awaken to my divine Goddess identity; to return to a God-Goddess's heart; to activate my light body through dancing and meditating; to be a new illumined human; to find my divine mission; to write about the higher truth and spread the light of hope and joy; to prepare for the final Twin Flame reunion; to become the divine instrument of the Great Spirit!"

The unbelievable mystical prophecy had been beautifully fulfilled. I recalled a diary entry I had written shortly after my arrival in Denmark.

February 4th, 2013, 23:31 p.m., in my bedroom
"Why have things become even more meaningless? I don't know why I came here! But strangely enough, even now, there's a picture of a woman appearing in my mind. She is loving and powerful, full of appreciation of the Great One; as if she has found out all the secrets and everything her soul has been longing for. She is divinely beautiful, smiling in light, doing her special work for the world, meaningfully and joyfully..."

Yes, I now understand. When I was in great pain and confusion, across time and space, my future self was transmitting her love and light to me, reassuring me that one day I would find all the precious treasures I deserved.

Chapter 28

Wounds and Thoughts

*I*n the middle of November, I wrote in my diary: "Concerning going home, I feel very good and happy about it. I feel I am successful. I didn't act as a victim and a coward—I did not cancel my trip, but instead I fought with my little self and I broke the limitations I had set for myself. I successfully defeated those weak and small energies that I had been carrying with me for such a long time!"

As the bigger picture of my life became clearer to me, a deeper level of healing occurred. I was forced to go back to my childhood and youth, to heal the deep buried wounds by re-living and re-shaping them. I recalled that when I was six years old, because of poverty my parents had to leave me and my sister at home to go to work in a factory in Guangzhou. I remembered one night I was holding my mother tightly, afraid that she would disappear when I woke up, because I knew that she and my father would take the train to Guangzhou the following day.

I woke up in the middle of the night and discovered that my parents had gone. Feeling terrified and saddened, a deep sense of loss got hold of me and I started to sob. It was the first time in my life that I had experienced the pain of separation.

For the next couple of years my sister and I lived with my father's parents. My grandfather had a kind heart, but a cold face. He rarely smiled or looked at us with love. In those days I was young, but sensitive; in his eyes I saw the hardships of his own life, his hidden blame toward my parents and all the unhappiness and heaviness he carried deep within.

I was very afraid of him. One night, I ran back to my parents' house accompanied by my young friends because deep down I felt I was unloved and unappreciated by my grandparents. I felt I was a worthless person and an undesired burden.

In middle school I was very good at Mandarin and English, but poor at math, physics and chemistry. During one class, my physics teacher asked me to go to the blackboard to draw an electrical circuit. I failed to do it because I had never really understood it. The teacher was upset with me and my poor performance and he punished me by asking me not to sit down in my seat but to stand up for the rest of the class.

I felt humiliated and wished I could somehow disappear, especially since it was a big class of 50 students. He looked at me with eyes full of reproach and disappointment. I lowered my head, feeling even more embarrassed.

During my years in high school, my parents came back home from Guangzhou and decided to grow rice to make a living, while supporting me and my sister so that we could go to school.

The toughest years were ahead of us. Poverty, hard work in the fields, unkind neighbors' words and actions led my parents to often quarrel. I witnessed their screams, shouts, hurts and fights. I felt my mother's deep pain and I cried with her; I sensed my father's helplessness and I ached for him. Seeing them arguing with each other with harsh words and sometimes physically fighting with each other made my heart feel painful and fearful. I cried in sorrow and trembled in horror.

I didn't enjoy my time at high school because I didn't like any other subjects except English. All year round I wore drab and cheap clothes, especially in winter, when I never had any really warm clothes or shoes to wear. I didn't compare myself with other pupils who seemed to enjoy material prosperity; neither did I blame my parents; instead, I felt deeply grateful for their hard work because they had done their best to help me change my destiny.

However, as a young girl, deep down I felt heavy and lonely. I saw myself as an ugly duckling and I developed a poor self image.

I came to realize that those deep seated fears, hurts and feelings of unworthiness had been buried deep inside me for many years. The wounds of my soul had never been acknowledged or healed until I met Oskar and came to Denmark. Then my false beliefs about myself and the world were finally erased.

I told myself to forgive my grandfather, my teacher and my parents' unloving quarrels, understanding that I had chosen to experience those hurts before this incarnation, because through them I needed to learn some important soul lessons. I let all the sadness and tears go with love; I blessed them all with love; I rewrote the history with love. In love we forgive and are re-born with total freedom and mercy.

November 21st, 2013, morning, at the library
A lot of thanks to the Great Spirit and all the loving guidance I have received during this journey. And I know you are with me always. Please continue guiding me till I reach my highest potential and goals.

Recently, I feel that my third eye is awakening and getting stronger day by day. I have been wondering when it will finally completely open. And by the way, what am I going to use my fully awakened third eye to do?

I am going to see what kind of hurts and fears have become stuck in people's subconscious causing their limited thoughts and destructive thinking patterns. And I am going to release them! And also, it would be very inspiring to see people's highest potentials, for example, their life purposes.

So, being a writer and a healer is possible! And of course, I can also join some dance clubs or find some ways to further develop my dancing skills! And I am sure that my next big task is to write my book! So far, it is perhaps the best thing I can do for humanity now!

November 28th, 2013, 6 p.m., in my bedroom
Dear Spirits, May you keep my heart and spirit shining and pure; may you help me to grow to the fullest and the best I can be.

At this moment, I feel like writing down all the beautiful aspects of my beloved Oskar, even though there is no way he can read or acknowledge these words. No matter how many faults he finds in himself, he is still the apple of my eye.

Darling Oskar, you are a very loving, gentle, funny, expressive, creative, honest, sincere, handsome, original, and charming man. I knew you a long, long time ago. I now send you love and light, my beloved.

Here comes an important question: as women, how can we make our lives really work?

By sitting quietly, listening to our inner voices and activating our innate Goddess's identity; by dancing, by meditating, and by sharing time with the greater self!

Everyone has more strength than realized by their ego. Keep following your path and one day you will reach the rainbow.

December 4th, 16:30 p.m., in my bedroom
Last night I had an interesting dream; it was a good one.

I was riding a motorbike in a tunnel, and then, I saw an orange cat standing in my way. I didn't hit her, but I let her safely go. The tunnel was under a bridge. I felt quite tired and I did not want to continue riding to the end, so I rode back to my home town, where I was happy to greet my grandmother and my sister.

I checked online where I read that to dream of an orange cat means that I have found my feminine side of creativity, sexuality, and power.

I feel very good about it.

I can sense that everything is coming to an end. I have brought this Danish adventure to an early close because I feel that this particular door cannot lead me anywhere further. And, living here alone isn't necessarily so satisfying any more. But this experience has taught me so many important things. Thanks! Thanks to all the people who have loved and helped me along the way! Everything that has happened feels like a dream.

I am leaving with a joyful and grateful spirit!

Chapter 29

Goodbye Denmark; See You Next Time!

On Thursday, December 5th, I went to the local town and bought a gift for Mette and Thomas—a set of three small lovely vases. At 6 p.m., as usual, we started to eat dinner together. Thomas and Mette had been invited by their friends to go to a party on the following day. So it was our last dinner before I was supposed to be leaving Denmark.

My gift for them was a lovely surprise, as was theirs. They gave me a beautiful heart-shaped candle holder from George Jenson, a nice Danish brand. But what really touched me was the loving sentiment from Mette: "DeDe, it means that you are in our hearts."

As you will always be in mine, dear Mette, Thomas, Sofus and Tobias.

Friday, December 6th was my last working day as an au pair. I got up around 6:30 a.m. and started to do everything in a special mood. I cleaned around the house carefully, reflecting... "There, right there, I used to cry; here, right here, I used to feel the pain." This house, every corner of it, has witnessed my pain and my joy. But tomorrow, I will be leaving. I just felt like saying, "Thank you, thank you for everything!"

After finishing my work, it was already 3 p.m. How much I wanted to bike to the lovely town of Ribe to say goodbye to my friends and my beloved forest! But there was a storm outside and I could see no one riding a bike on the road. I felt upset about the weather and wondered what I could do about it.

Feeling a bit bored, I started to pack. A few minutes later, I heard someone knocking at the door. I wondered who it was, who had come to our house on such a stormy day.

I was shocked and surprised. The man who had come to the house was one of the local volunteers who had been teaching us Danish for the past months. He was a nice old Danish man whose name I didn't even know, but who had been so kind and helpful. I remembered that he had generously bought us nice gifts; mine was a lovely rainbow-colored handbag.

He said he knew I would be leaving on the following day and he wanted to say goodbye and wish me a pleasant journey. Meanwhile, he gave me an envelope, inside of which was a lovely hand-written card and 500 Danish Kroner.

I was deeply touched to receive his gifts; tears immediately came to my eyes. I wanted to thank him for his kindness, so I gave him the red colored fish toy I had brought from Beijing. He accepted it with much joy.

After saying goodbye to him, I resumed my packing.

Soon my friend Benny called; he reproached me for not having contacted him and not having asked him to pick me up to give me a ride. I explained that I didn't want to bother him. In the end, he said he would come back within half an hour. I felt happy to hear that.

I asked Benny to drive me to the nearby forest because I wanted to say goodbye to my dancing oasis, and to thank it for all the beauty and power it had brought into my life.

Once there, I whispered to the spirit of the forest: "One day, I will return with my beloved other half and I will dance here again. We have shared so many lovely afternoons here; you have watched my movements and felt my deepest feelings; you encouraged me to move on and evolve; you know who I really am and who I will eventually become. I now understand the journey I am on and I am making my destiny come true. One day, we will see each other again."

Before driving to Benny's house I received an unexpected phone call from Mrs. Ellen, one of the organizers of the center for volunteers—a kind and loving Danish lady. She said she knew I would be leaving the next day and she wanted to say goodbye. I felt happy and excited to hear that. Within a few minutes, Benny and I arrived at her house.

Warm hugs, lovely coffee, home-made cookies, plus a gift for me. I felt deeply touched and grateful. My gift was the book, *The Ugly Duckling* by Hans Christian Anderson. What a special gift!

I heard my heart thinking, "This book is actually telling my story! I was that poor, small, ugly duckling before! Until I came here and experienced all of this, and finally came to understand that I am a divine, lovely swan!

"Look! The last page of this book says that the beautiful swan has finally found her true companions and they are enjoying themselves, full of joy and elegance, on the spring lake!"

After saying goodbye to Ellen, Benny and I drove to his house. For the last time, I enjoyed his music CD, his artistic collection, his lovely flowers etc. As usual, our conversation happily continued, accompanied by lovely food and music.

I told Benny about my thoughts of writing a book; he encouraged me to do it and believed I would make it happen. I also told him that one day I would come back to Denmark and I would definitely see him again. He said he looked forward to it very much.

It was only a few minutes' walk from Benny's house to Shela's shop. Around 7 p.m. I went to the shop, as previously agreed with Shela. Sheila not only gave me a big loving hug but also a few presents, which I liked a lot.

I thanked Shela and told her I would come back to Denmark to see her again. She believed me and smiled warmly.

Afterwards, Benny drove me home. It was time to say goodbye.

"DeDe, you are a very brave person. I truly admire the things you do. You came so far to pursue your dream and I wish you well. Take good care of yourself. I know you will realize all your dreams. I wish

The Twin Flame Lover of China and Denmark

you all the best! One day, we will see each other again."

"Benny, you are such a lovely friend. You invited me to the forest and the island; you let me see the beautiful fairy tale side of Denmark, which I will never forget. How lucky I am to have met you. You are sincere, funny, sunny and positive. I also wish you all the best. We will see each other again!"

Benny left. By then, it was 8 p.m., or so. I spent some time cleaning and packing. By the time I had finished everything, it was almost midnight, and I fell asleep, feeling happy and content.

The following day was December 7th; Mette and Thomas had come back from the party. At 10 a.m. Thomas was supposed to drive me to the train station while Mette was going to stay at home with Sofus and Tobias.

The moment to bid each other farewell had arrived. A very unexpected feeling had risen up within me; it felt hard to leave this kind family. With tears in my eyes, I said goodbye to Mette and apologized for everything one more time. Mette cheered me up by saying, "DeDe, you have really done very well. You are not annoying at all. We have been living in the same house and sometimes it is unavoidable that there are conflicts, as we each have our own problems or moments of distress. You take great care of yourself and have a safe journey! We will see you again!"

I was touched to hear that. I thought about the good times we had shared, the delicious apple cake she used to make, the nice comments she would make about my Danish and the interesting conversations we had had. I felt happy, as I said to her, "Mette, take care! I will definitely see you again!"

Half an hour later I arrived at the train station. Before getting on the train, I said to Thomas, "Thank you, Thomas, for your kindness and warmth. You know, the CD player you found for me changed my whole destiny. I used it to play many CDs and I have started to dance. You might think your kindness is small, but to me it is huge. Thanks a lot!"

With his usual modesty and kindness, Thomas replied, "DeDe, you are more than welcome."

Sitting on the train, I felt peaceful and happy, for my life in a cave was finally over, after some important necessary inner work had been successfully achieved.

My friend Jette came to the train station to pick me up. I was delighted to see her again after such a long time. We had a lovely lunch together to celebrate my "graduation." After our conversation and a walk, it became 6 p.m. So we then took the train to her parents' house to stay there for the night.

The following day, Jette and I got up quite early in the morning and hurried to Ane and Harold's house in Copenhagen.

"Dear DeDe! Congratulations! You made it! You survived! I am so proud of you!" said Ane.

I told Ane I would turn my story into a book after returning to Beijing and I would visit Copenhagen to see her again.

It felt unbelievable to Ane, but she still encouraged me enthusiastically, saying that she very much looked forward to me achieving my goals.

After the short visit, Jette and I hurried to Copenhagen Airport.

"Jette, thank you so much for your lovely company. I will definitely write my book and come back to see you again. We will enjoy ourselves on the lovely streets of Copenhagen again!"

"Yes. I trust you will. We will see each other again. I will await your arrival. Take good care and have a safe journey. Email me when you arrive in Beijing!"

Sitting at the airport, waiting for the plane departure, I felt safe and centered. I sensed my power and strength. I was calm and confident and I heard an inner voice saying, "Well done, congratulations! One journey is over, a new one begins."

STAGE SIX

Soul's Realization—Becoming Radiant (January 2014-July 2016)

*A*s one listens to the heart and continuously engages in self-realization, moving toward the fulfillment of the soul, the surrendered twin is guided to wake up to her higher powers of healing and her innate God-Given gifts... She becomes a divine channel of the Great Light and walks upon her highest soul's path; she continues emitting her special starlight for the benefit of others. By offering soul-level service and sharing soul-level love, the gateway of the heart begins to open...

Chapter 30

What Happened to Santiago in "The Alchemist"?

After having a recurring dream about finding his treasure in the pyramids in Egypt, Santiago, the dream boy in *The Alchemist*, decided to follow his dream. After many tests and challenges, he finally reached the pyramids.

However, when he arrived there, he got beaten and robbed by two bandits. The pyramids were not where his treasure was buried. In the end, he realized where his treasure lay. It was right in the abandoned church where he had that recurring dream!

It was quite an unexpected ending for me and I actually felt puzzled about it. However, as life went on, I gradually began to understand the philosophy behind it.

Surprisingly, I also walked Santiago's path and had then returned to "the abandoned church," which for me was the Beijing Double Happiness Courtyard Hotel, where I found my treasure.

I arrived in Beijing from Denmark on December 9th, 2013. After two short days in Beijing I went home, a place I had been missing very much.

My parents almost immediately recognized that I had changed. Two weeks later, my father said to me, "Since your return from Denmark you seem like you have grown a lot. You are much more mature and considerate than before. Most importantly, you get up much earlier. This means you have finally realized the importance of time. We feel very happy about it. The risk you had taken has clearly paid off."

"Dad, as you had predicted, initially I didn't really find any happiness there. But later on I found my true self."

After two weeks' of relaxing time at home I started to think seriously about writing my book. Despite my fears and doubts, I began to write it a week later. I didn't have any confidence in my English writing ability back then and so at the beginning I started writing my book in Mandarin.

While writing, I was also struggling to find a nice job in Beijing on the Internet. However, after much searching I could not find any jobs that interested me. I still missed my old job at the Double Happiness Courtyard hotel and I wondered if I should contact my old boss Oliver, or not.

I thought about the many advantages I would gain in terms of working hours, payment, days off, etc., if I got my old job back. In particular, I realized my work hours would enable me to have a lot of time to write my book. Even though I worried about what people there might think of me, in the end I listened to my heart and decided to return, feeling that a strange force was attracting me back.

I arrived in Beijing on February 12th, 2014. Two days later I contacted Oliver regarding the possibility of working at the hotel again. With his usual encouragement, Oliver said that I was more than welcome. On February 16th I came back to the Double Happiness Courtyard hotel and started working there.

My co-workers, managers and the housekeeping ladies recognized the changes in me and said to me, "DeDe! You have changed! I can't explain how exactly, but you have become a totally different person; DeDe, before you went to Denmark you were like a sweet little girl, but now you have become a mature young lady, very unbelievable; DeDe, I feel you are much more grounded and centered now. It is truly a great transformation. I feel deeply happy for you."

Two weeks later I continued my writing, fully aware that I was in a stage of balancing myself and summarizing the past, that the most important things I needed, were to develop myself further, and continue my dancing, meditating and writing.

I cheered myself up by writing in my diary, "Shela knows who I really am and who I can become. My higher self and my dear soul also know. Keep the faith and the fire. I will try to uplift others by my peace and higher purpose, instead of being affected by lower minds and thoughts. I can grow joyfully!"

From the middle of March to August, the rhythm of my life was as follows:

Day one: Working from 8 a.m. to 8 p.m. as a receptionist.

Day two: Writing from 10 a.m. to 6 or 7 p.m. as a writer, working from 8 p.m. to 8 a.m. on the night shift (we do get a few hours of sleep during the night shift).

Day three: After the night shift I would sleep during the day and relax. I would not write or work, but I would dance for one or two hours in the evening.

Day four: A full day off. Writing from 9 a.m. to 6 or 7 p.m. and dancing for two hours in the evening.

A life like that felt repetitive, yet constructive and meaningful. Living consciously with my life purposes, I felt fulfilled and satisfied.

My co-workers and I did not really share any common interests or likes. Therefore, I sometimes felt rather alone. However, I reminded myself to try my best to thank them for their energy, which contributed to my growth. Deep down I knew they were yearning for growth and they, too, had their own inner light, waiting to become activated.

I thought about my beloved Oskar frequently, or rather, I missed him a lot, a lot, a lot. When I was not dancing or writing, I often wondered how his life had been and if he had totally forgotten about me or not. It excited me to imagine what his feelings would be if I told him about my journey and growth. I assumed he would feel very happy and proud of me and that our hearts would dance together in our shared deep joy and honor.

The Twin Flame Lover of China and Denmark

I also fantasized about our eventual reunion and what we could do after finally coming together. In my imagination I often saw us joyfully traveling and working together, sharing our values and our mission; that we were living a New Age lifestyle with colorful love and light.

Sometimes I believed it could become true some day; at other times I felt that I was merely living with an impossible illusion. Nevertheless, I never thought about contacting him. My heart and soul were not ready.

Time moved quickly to August. By that time I had finished writing the Mandarin version of this book. I felt relieved and happy. The very first thing that came to my mind was to create a better life for myself by publishing the book in China.

During the whole of September I spent most of my time contacting publishers, sending my book sample to them, meeting editors, etc. However, due to the immaturity of the book or, for whatever other reasons, I did not succeed in publishing it, and I gradually gave up on the idea, telling myself to be patient and to wait for the right time to act upon it.

On October 22nd, one of my co-workers quit her job and left our hotel. Her bed was located in a rather spacious and private area in our shared dormitory and after she left I was able to move into her space; I wondered how I could make the best use of this good advantage.

For the next whole week I relaxed into a routine, which didn't bring me any sense of true joy, but only a kind of boredom, and prompted feelings of meaninglessness. However, at one point I thought to myself, "Maybe I can type up my English diaries on the computer? The diaries written in Denmark are very important and inspirational! And maybe I can even write my book in English."

The idea scared me to some extent because I told myself I would never make it, since English is not my native language. However, a strong impulse led me to start clearing up my diaries by typing them into my computer.

During this process my main thoughts were, "If Oskar is not coming back to reunite with me, then what am I going to do with my life? No other man can ever take his place in my heart. So, I had better go to a convent and live a simple life there. No, that sounds lonely and sad! Moreover, my wonderful talents of speaking English, communicating with people, dancing, healing and writing would all be wasted! No, no, to serve God or Buddha by going to a convent is definitely not the right way for me!"

Waiting is very hard to do. My heart was suffering. "Does Oskar still love me, or not? What am I to him in his life? Am I simply a lost memory of his past, or the real home of his soul? Such a long time has passed and I have heard nothing from him. What actual facts are supporting my belief that one day he will return? In reality we are drifting further and further away from each other's life, since we are completely out of touch, and perhaps, out of love? But yet, I know deep down I am still waiting, waiting for the rainbow time of our reunion."

Life without the one you love is like a candle with no perfume.

But there is still one very important and beautiful thing one can do, that is, to be one with our spirit and soul. You look upward. You know that there is something higher than you, higher than life, leading and uplifting you. Your eyes cannot see it, but there is no doubt that you can feel it. And you hold on to it.

I love myself. I find myself most fulfilled when I dance; I find peace, clarity, comfort, as well as my own center when I write and read; I bathe in light and depth when I meditate.

"Keep doing these important things! Keep transforming and evolving!"

By the end of 2014 I had finished typing all my English diaries on the computer and I wondered what I should do next.

At the beginning of January, 2015 I heard the inner call to write my book in English and also the urge to contact some dear friends whom I had not emailed for a long time due to my busy days. One of them was my special friend Wendy, whom I had met in my hotel in 2012.

Wendy is from England and had worked as a French and German teacher for many years in schools. She likes reading, teaching and traveling and has a wide range of interests, such as gardening, cooking, history, cultural differences, etc. Even though she is much older than me, it has never bothered us or prevented us from sharing our interests and our deep understanding of each other.

I felt it had been a deep blessing to have met her and we had become dear friends. Neither of us imagined that she would be, later on, the first special reader and editor of this book.

I told Wendy about my plan to write this book in English. She felt quite impressed to hear that and said that she would very much like to read it. That excited me and it gave me a more powerful motivation to complete writing it.

January 18th, 2015 I started writing the first chapter of my book. From then on, the rhythm of my life became something similar to what it was like when I was writing this book in Mandarin: working, writing, relaxing, dancing, meditating, etc.

During this period my main thoughts were, "The dream must continue. I ride a brave horse called courage, guided by faith and perseverance, lightened by love and trust, running freely on the great path of self-realization. My only purpose and intention is to be fulfilled and let the divine mission be successfully completed.

"Of course, I want so much to be in love, to see, hug, and kiss Oskar again, or even to build a happy family with him, give birth to our child and live a beautiful life together, as I have always dreamed about. But no, I cannot do this right now. Reality dictates that I need to complete my mission first. Only after writing this book, would the divine opportunity and the divine possibility of reuniting with each other be possible.

"Every day, there are tragedies and crimes occurring in the world. But we should not let them destroy or drain our energy. More importantly, we should not let them stop us from doing the beautiful things we are meant to do. Our sorrow or bad feelings about them cannot change the world. However, it is our great work, be it writing or performing any other type of service, or making a contribution from the heart, that can transform and change one human's mind forever. And this is the true way for our world to become a better place—by shining our light.

"Recently I have been wondering whether Oskar will eventually return or not. How much I wish we could complete our mission together by me doing the writing and he the illustrating! He is such a talented artist and I adore his beautiful drawings! God, if we could work together, imagine how wonderful that would be! How loving that sounds! And if that were to happen, that would probably astound our friends! Our parents, friends, all the people who know us would definitely be deeply uplifted by our reunion! They would be amazed by the unbelievable charm of it!

"But the important question is: will Oskar be back?

"I don't know. We will see. Please help me publish my book and bring my Oskar back!

"One of the deep reasons why I feel so energized and inspired to continue writing is because of my dear friend Wendy. She has been reading my book. I have been emailing the chapters to her as soon as I finish them. She is an important supporter in the shadows and is a very powerful and influential force involved in all that I do. I will always remember her for her invaluable love and support."

Time flew quickly, within the rhythm of writing and working, as I continued sharing thoughts and feelings with Wendy. On May 22nd, the first version of my book was finished, ending with the description of my departure from Denmark.

Almost at the same time, one of my co-workers left our hotel. As a result, I had to take over her shift schedule which was quite different from mine. Since then, I began working for two days from 8 a.m. to 10 p.m., and then having time off for two days. Not having to do any night shifts, I felt rather better and happier.

That sudden change actually felt quite strange to me and I thought to myself, "Coincidence? Or another timely event? As soon as I finished writing my book, my co-worker left! This is a brand new start in my life! What will happen next?"

Chapter 31

One Hour Conversation With Oskar

After finishing writing the book I actually didn't experience the feeling of completion that I had expected. Was it because Oskar's heart still had not returned to me or because I had not yet totally fulfilled myself as a writer, dancer and healer?

The answer was: both.

I was still missing him a lot, but I knew I should not get mired in this position; instead, I should always move on, keeping my deepest love for him within myself.

I listened to my inner urge to get a driver's license and at the beginning of June I signed up for the course.

The rhythm of my life had changed to working, dancing and combining theory and practical classes in preparation for my driver's license test. It was busy and productive, but in a corner of my mind I was thinking, "After this period, I will have to seriously figure out some ways to fulfill myself!"

After much training and hard work I successfully passed my driver's test at the end of September. I felt a sense of joy and pride in my accomplishment. But at the same time, I felt quite lost about what to do next. I was sure I wanted to fulfill myself, but I just couldn't see clearly which way to go.

I thought about contacting Oskar at this time, even though deep down I knew I wasn't ready. However, I needed an answer and I desperately wanted to know how he had been feeling about us. I expected a different reaction from him, because I knew I had changed and was now very different from before.

Before I finally contacted him, I made a list of my fears in my diary.

"He will probably laugh at my craziness and foolishness, that after so many years I still love him so much; I am afraid of being rejected and feeling hurt again, just like last time; I deeply fear to hear that he has already moved on and is now living happily with someone else."

Back then, I had been unconsciously vibrating with such low and dense energies of fears, which, according to the eternal universal Law of Attraction, were inevitably manifesting into the very reality I had feared.

On October 20th, around 7 p.m., regardless of all my deep fears, I ignored my reservations and dialed his phone number.

DeDe: "Hi, Oskar."

Oskar: "Oh hi, is that DeDe?"

DeDe: "Yes it is. I just wanted to say hi. How are you?"

Oskar: "It's really a surprise to hear from you. I mean, this is very good. I've been very well. How are you? Where are you now?"

DeDe: "Yes, it is a surprise for me, too. I mean, I never thought about contacting you again, but recently I have felt like calling you. Originally I thought about writing an email, but in the end I decided to call you directly."

Oskar: "I agree. This feels better than emailing. You sound very well; it feels like you are much more grounded. Are you still in Beijing?"

DeDe: "Yes, I am. After coming back from Denmark I returned to my old hotel to work. Very unbelievable. I know you will think that as well. I just wanted to say hi to you, nothing serious. I need to hang up now because I am using my hotel's phone to call you and it is very expensive."

Oskar: "Actually, I am now eating my lunch. But do you mind if I call you back in about ten minutes' time?"

DeDe: "Okay, I will wait. We will talk then."

The Twin Flame Lover of China and Denmark

As I hung up the phone, I felt excited. I sensed your joy to hear from me after such a long time and I felt happy that you seemed to recognize my transformation, just by listening to my voice. We were talking in a relaxed, and warm, or even joyful way.

All these good signs made my heart start to dance happily and it brought back the sweet and loving sensations I used to experience when we were still together a few years ago. I even started to fantasize about the possibility of us getting back together again.

However, things took a crazy, cruel turn when you called me back.

Oskar: "Hey, it's really nice to hear from you, but I must tell you that I moved on a long time ago and I've been seeing someone else recently, someone whom I have strong feelings about. We are not boyfriend or girlfriend yet, but I see we are going to be; it's been going very well."

Another soul-destroying, crushing blow! I found myself uncontrollably trembling in unspeakable pain when hearing those words from you. I couldn't believe my deepest fears had become the cruelest truth. I was totally devastated, feeling deeply, deeply hurt.

As tears welled up in my eyes, I thought, "Why have things become like this? Isn't Oskar my Twin Flame? Is everything I believed about Twin Flames all wrong? Or have I just been too stubborn and unwilling to accept that he has truly moved on? What has been really happening?"

I then acted rather aggressively, motivated by anger and jealousy.

DeDe: "Okay, that sounds very fine, very good! What is she like? Tell me all her good points."

Oskar: "This really sounds a bit absurd, but okay–she is good, very good. She is sensitive, reasonable, has empathy..."

DeDe: "Fine! Stop! I don't want to hear any more!"

If only you knew about my growth and discovery about the Twin Flames, you would be able to fully understand how I was feeling at that moment. I wanted to shout at you like a crazed, angry tiger, but

I knew it would not change anything. Therefore, I forced myself to calm down. Bitterly, I blurted out, "Fine, I hope you two break up soon. You will experience a horrible relationship."

Oskar: "No no, you cannot say things like that."

DeDe: "Why not? Should I say, 'I hope you two stay together forever,' when in fact, you are the one I still care about?"

Oskar: "No, you cannot..."

I then realized I was perhaps thinking only of myself, so I changed my approach.

DeDe: "Okay, I admit, it was not very good to say something like that; I take my words back. Since we've come to this point already, I'd like to ask you why you didn't contact me after we had said goodbye last time..."

Oskar: "Because you gave me the impression that I should only contact you if I wanted to be with you. And you know it is not like that; our approaches are different. Our minds fit well together, but our reality doesn't allow us to be together! I am not prepared to move to China and you cannot move to Denmark. Besides, so many years have passed and most probably we have both changed a lot.

"Sometimes I imagined that if you were in Denmark and if we could see each other, we could probably have been together. It is the distance between us which makes our situation rather difficult and complicated.

"And may I ask, why didn't you contact me afterwards? Why do you always expect me to be the first one to make the contact?"

Hearing all this I felt angry and I judged you to be lacking in courage, not daring to challenge our reality. Then I realized that I was equally at fault in this respect.

For a long time our focus had always been, "It's so difficult, the distance between us..." We never thought about our situation as a positive challenge: "It is indeed not easy, but what can we do to change it together? How can we transform the impossible into a miracle?"

At that moment, I hated myself for always appearing to be the one

The Twin Flame Lover of China and Denmark

to push and force things to occur, instead of patiently following the flow.

I thought to myself, "The fact that I didn't contact you doesn't mean I stopped loving you! I wasn't ready!"

In reality, I said, "I didn't contact you because I've been very busy writing a book!"

Oskar: "What?! You have been writing a book?"

DeDe: "The book is about us! It is our story!"

Hearing this, you felt rather shocked, but in a good way. You even laughed a bit in response to your contradicting emotions.

Oskar: "Wow, if the book gets published, you must let me know; I want to read it."

I was thinking, "My original purpose was to get you back by writing this book, but now I see that is not going to work. I don't want to feel deeply embarrassed or hurt again!"

Therefore, I said, "No no, I won't let you know and I won't send it to you!"

Oskar: "Come on, why not? I want to read it! By the way, did you go back to Beijing after we said goodbye?"

DeDe: "No, I did not. I thought I would, but I actually stayed in Denmark for eleven months."

Oskar: "What? You said you were going home afterwards!"

DeDe: "It doesn't make any sense to argue about this now. By the way, have you heard of the term 'Twin Flame'?"

Oskar: "Twin Flame? You mean something like soul mates, or what? No, I have never heard of that."

I realized that somehow we had been walking on two very different paths regarding our perceptions about our relationship and there were significant distances between these paths. Obviously, like the old me, you had not recognized the sacred nature of our relationship.

At that moment I felt extremely confused about why destiny would only reveal the Twin Flame secret to me, but not you. I started to doubt everything I had believed about the Twin Flame idea.

Feeling rather drained, I said, "Yes, you can understand it like that. I guess we have said all we need to say, right? Maybe it's time to hang up now. I wish you well. You take care."

Oskar: "Yes, I guess so, too. I feel like saying, it's really nice to hear from you. You take care."

DeDe: "Thanks. Goodbye."

Oskar: "Bye."

I hung up the phone. I kept trembling in pain for a few minutes, and tears of sorrow streamed down my face.

That same night I didn't go to bed until 1 a.m. and I woke up around 5 a.m., because I just couldn't sleep any more. I made the resolution to do whatever I could to publish my book and meanwhile find my way to fulfill myself as a healer and a dancer. Only in this way could all the pain and hurt and everything I had undertaken be justified.

Back then, my understanding of the whole story was: "Everything that happened is truly a cruel joke! The divine Twin Flame idea probably exists but it's just that Oskar and I are not true Twin Flames! Otherwise, things wouldn't have turned out like this. It's time for me to totally forget about it and move on!"

It was only many months later, after being guided to read Kathleen Cranton's Twin Flame teachings, that my understanding shifted into a rather different direction. "Oskar still can be my true Twin Flame. For the past few years I had been constantly healing and raising my vibration through dancing and meditating, etc. As a result, Oskar's and my shared energy must have increased and I believe that subconsciously we had been accelerating the reunion process.

The fact that he was attracted into another relationship is not necessarily a bad thing. To a large extent it can be a karmic relationship he is meant to experience, or has to address before he can fully, freely and totally commit himself to our relationship. In another way, it is actually helping and assisting our final reunion.

Perhaps that relationship will eventually help him to clearly see his heart and soul...

Twin Flames are said to be each other's greatest helpmates. They seek to completely fulfill each other by raising their levels of consciousness and completing their soul missions; most of the time it's done in a positive way through soul-level inspiration and encouragement. But when it is necessary, or when the time is right, this universe will arrange their relationship differently, in its own way, according to its divine plan and grand vision.

In our case, it could be that when I got stuck, not knowing how to truly fulfill myself as a writer, dancer and healer, the powerful energies of anger and resentment I felt caused by Oskar's karmic relationship were meant to help me by forcing me to reach my goals..."

Now, here comes the big suspense: "Which explanation will prove to be true in the future?"

I don't know. Let's follow the flow, continue reading and see.

Chapter 32

Becoming a Writer

A few important changes happened after my conversation with Oskar. The first small but meaningful one was that I gave myself a new English name; before I was called DeDe or Miss Wan as a reception manager in our hotel. However, I decided to have a new beginning and I followed my heart to call myself Indigo. This name had resonated with me since the first time I saw this word.

It not only marked my desire to stand out to the world with a totally new identity, but also expressed my deep wish to become someone significant in the future. My mind was thinking, "Since I have failed seriously in my love affair, it makes perfect sense for me to win in other areas of my life, right? I cannot always be a loser in every field I touch, right? I was born to be a shining star instead of a miserable loser!"

Indigo, the special name, which I like a lot, has since then been remembered and appreciated by people I meet. It has proved to be a successful and popular change, which makes me feel quite happy.

The next important issue of my heart was about my book. How to really get it published and where to find the right publisher? What was lacking and how should I complete the last step toward fulfilling my soul's mission?

I thought to myself, "English is, after all, not my native language, I need someone, a special one to help me edit this book. After the editing, I will then start thinking about the publishing issue. But

The Twin Flame Lover of China and Denmark

how and where can I find that special important editor?"

Originally I thought about hiring some native English speaker in Beijing to help with the editing and I even met and talked with a few of them. But it didn't work out. Some merely came for the money and others were lacking in integrity and competence. Just when I was about to give up, I suddenly realized that that special one could have always been with me! My dear friend Wendy!

"Wendy is a native English speaker and has worked as a French and German teacher for many years. Besides, she likes reading books and traveling a lot. She is not only competent in her excellent language skills, but also has an open mindset. Most importantly, she has read my story once and she understands my heart as a dear friend! She is the perfect editor I've been looking for! WOW!"

My heart raced with great excitement as I was thinking those thoughts. Shortly afterwards, I emailed Wendy and asked her if she would like to help with the editing.

"Dear Indigo, yes! I would be glad to help you with the editing!"

Wendy's cheerful reply made my heart dance happily. A magical and meaningful journey shared between us was about to begin.

After our discussion, Wendy helped condensing the first three original chapters into one new chapter and suggested changing the sequence of the first two chapters. This was a very good suggestion and I totally agreed. She also advised me to go through the book again to see how I felt about it from my current state of mind.

It was my turn to do something. As I was reading the original version, I clearly recognized that there were too many ego-based perceptions and expressions involved; such energy would not be inspiring to the reader and risked making people feel drained.

It was not a high level mature version, not the one my soul wanted to deliver to the world for the purpose of uplifting and empowering others. In other words, it needed to be re-written with a much higher and more compassionate consciousness.

Thinking about rewriting the book, I wanted to run away from the demanding work that I had imagined it would require from me, but I knew that the longer I postponed it, the more pain I would feel. "When it comes to obeying the command of our soul and fulfilling our divine mission, the word 'free will' is just a delusional concept."

I read this sentence somewhere and I remembered it firmly in my heart. No more excuses or delays, I must simply do it today, do it now.

Some time in early February, Wendy and I officially started the editing journey.

For two days from 7:30 a.m. to 9:30 p.m. I would work as an English-speaking reception manager in my hotel, living in the business world and earning my living. For the following two days off I would write from 8 a.m. to 5 p.m. each day (of course there were short breaks in between), living in another world, made of colors and dreams.

I set myself the aim of re-writing one chapter per day. For the first few chapters the process felt slow and I was unaccustomed to this kind of work, but once the channel was open, I gradually found my way and was able to ride the flow.

Every time I finished re-writing one chapter, I would email it to Wendy for her further "polish." Within a few days Wendy then would email me the edited version and share her suggestions and advice with me, all aiming to help me improve and raise the level of not only my writing skills, but also my thinking patterns reflected in the writing.

Each time I read her polished version, I noted the places which had been perfectly corrected. I recognized how deeply Wendy cared about the work we were doing together. After we had edited each chapter, I began to feel I was getting closer and closer to my dreamland. And I have to tell you, it is a beautiful and truly fulfilling feeling!

This is the reason why, in the preface, I acknowledge Wendy as the important "supporter in the shadows" and as one of the most important forces involved in all that I do. Without her continuous soul-level love and support, this book would not be held in your hands today. Dear Wendy, thank you!

While the writing and editing was going on, I was constantly thinking, "How and where can I find the right publisher?"

After getting the approval of my manger Oliver, I wrote a brief introduction to my book on a piece of paper and put it on the information board in our reception area, aiming to attract some publishers or potential readers. However, this brought no results. Our guests never asked about it. I wondered whether this was because they were not interested, or whether my story simply felt strange or odd to them, so they didn't want to know anything about it.

I felt a bit discouraged, but not downhearted, as I had confidence in the light of my book, written with my heart and soul. Deep down, I wished and believed that some day, somehow, the miracle would happen in its own way.

A few days later, due to the renovation work in our reception area, the information board was taken down and as a result, there was nowhere to put my "publicity."

"Take a deep breath, let it be, let it be, the miracle will come in another way. Let's do one thing at a time. Now, please focus on the writing and the editing. What I need will come to me naturally. Take a deep breath..."

I had to positively calm and comfort myself in this way.

Some time around early March, after reading one edited chapter from Wendy, I felt quite confused about some sentences in the chapter. In order to figure it out, I decided to approach a native English speaker guest in our hotel to help me out.

Next day on my working shift I was attracted to ask an American lady named Joanna Infeld for her help.

Prior to this I had never exchanged any words with her, but I remembered that when I had first seen her face, I noticed her energy was high, calm and different from most people's.

The Twin Flame Lover of China and Denmark

It was early evening, and Joanna had ordered some food in our bar and was waiting for it to arrive. I thought it was a good time to ask my question and so I walked toward her, with the printed chapter in my hands. A short, funny but meaningful conversation took place:

Indigo: "Excuse me M'am, I know you are from America and you are a native English speaker. You speak great and perfect English! Do you mind helping me with something regarding English? I feel quite confused about some sentences here and I need to figure them out."

Joanna: "Oh, sure, my pleasure! Let me see..."

Joanna solved my puzzle and I felt quite grateful for her help. In the end, she asked, "Is this some kind of homework or assignment for your English studies?"

Indigo: "Oh, no! This is a very important chapter of my first book! I am a writer! My English friend is helping me with the editing and we are going to publish this book sooner or later!"

I was speaking of my writer identity and my first book with a huge sense of excitement and pride. I already knew that words have not only the power to demonstrate who we really are and who we want to become, but that also in turn they can shape our reality according to what we say and believe.

Joanna seemed surprised and delighted to hear that; perhaps she also felt somewhat amused. With light in her eyes, she cheerfully said to me: "Oh, very nice to meet you! I am also a writer, and a publisher. I would like to know more about your work..."

Hearing this, I became excited. I thought, "Dear God! She says she is not only a writer, but also a publisher! Could it be that she is the destined publisher for my book? Wow!"

During Joanna's stay I asked her many questions regarding writing and publishing. Her answers inspired me a lot and helped me realize that to publish a book was not necessarily the difficult struggle I originally thought it to be. During our conversations we also recognized the similarities of the work we do, that the essence

The Twin Flame Lover of China and Denmark

and the ultimate goal of our mission as a writer is to uplift, heal and empower people as much as we can.

A few days later we said farewell at the Beijing West Railway Station. We exchanged our email addresses and agreed to keep in touch.

The meeting was a deeply blessed meant-to-be encounter. Though things were not concrete at that time, I was almost sure that I had finally found the right publisher for my book.

By May 1st I had nearly finished re-writing all the chapters and Wendy had only a few chapters left to edit. I felt relieved and I started to think seriously about publishing the book.

A few days later I emailed Joanna and inquired about the possibility of publishing this book through her publishing company, Kora Press. To my great joy and excitement, Joanna not only said yes, but also offered me a special favorable price for the editing and publishing. I felt deeply grateful for this. Thank you, dear Joanna!

After a few months of editing and refinement, this book was finally published and is now being held in your hands.

I'd like to believe that during this journey of fulfilling myself as a writer, not only dear Wendy and Joanna have contributed much, but also the divine loving angels; I cannot see them with my eyes, but their presence has always felt close and dear to me. I know they exist in all of us and will always be our soul's companions, sending us their divine light and guidance.

Thank you, my dear angel friends.

Thank you, my dear readers.

Chapter 33

Becoming a Reiki Healer

*I*n chapter 17, I wrote, "My hand chakra is opening. I am perhaps awakening my healing ability. But in order to become a real healer, much training and practice will be needed. I have a long way to go…"

It has always been one of my deepest wishes to become a real healer. However, every time this longing came to my mind, I always deliberately put the thought away thinking, "Oh, no, I cannot become a healer, because it is such a "high-level title." I am afraid that I won't have the talent or gift to achieve such an accomplishment. I certainly want to become a healer, but I don't think there is anyone here in Beijing to teach me; therefore, it is not my fault. Maybe it would be easier and safer just to have this healer dream inside of me instead of actually realizing it… why bother with such things?"

All those excuses had suddenly disappeared after the conversation with Oskar. For the sake of justifying my lack of initiative, my thoughts were automatically transformed to, "I MUST become a healer! I MUST search everywhere I can to find a teacher to guide me onto my healing path! This is something I MUST do now!"

It became a burning desire. Whenever we have such a desire, it is very likely that we will attract what we want.

On October 22nd, 2015, two days after the conversation with Oskar, I sent a text message to ask my new friend Philip if he knew any Reiki healers or teachers in Beijing. To my great surprise and delight, he referred me to a lady named Erika, who was a Reiki student of a Reiki Master Teacher in Beijing.

Begonia is the Reiki Master Teacher, who soon afterwards became my Reiki teacher as well.

Wait a minute, who is Philip and how did I know him in Beijing? A rather interesting meant-to-be story had occurred much earlier.

One day around the middle of August, 2015, our hotel received a room inquiry email from a guest named Torben. From the phone number and his email address I knew he was from Denmark. "Denmark" – the special magical word immediately lit up my whole being. I felt inspired to be even more friendly than usual and I automatically started to write a few sentences in Danish in my emails to him.

I assumed Torben felt rather surprised to read my emails. However, out of politeness, he didn't directly ask me why I could write in Danish. However, he later wrote that he knew a Danish man who had been working and living in Beijing for a while; that if I would like to learn more Danish, he could introduce us to each other and we would see what could happen.

That was something I never expected. And to be honest, back then I was not really thinking of developing my Danish speaking skills. However, I felt touched by Torben's genuine kindness and I decided to give it a try.

Again, to my surprise, the Danish man mentioned in Torben's email was actually his son. Philip was a rather young and smart Danish man. After a few conversations with Philip I got the impression that he was not only energetic, but that he knew lots of people, especially westerners living in Beijing. I admired his courage to live abroad alone and his wide circle of friends.

That was how, completely out of the blue, I came to know Philip.

And then, after contacting Begonia a few times I concluded she was a trustworthy and respected teacher. I made up my mind to learn Reiki from her.

On December 12th and 13th I, together with another student, Angelika, completed the Reiki level one course in Begonia's apartment. Additionally, we each received an attunement four times (a ritual performed by the Reiki teacher to introduce Reiki energy to the student) from Begonia.

In order to better prepare ourselves as a clearer Reiki channel, we were assigned a homework of performing a Reiki self-treatment for 21 continuous days after the course, which would help purify our own energy.

A meaningful new ritual was introduced into my life. For the first 21 days, every night before going to bed, I performed Reiki on myself, and I liked it very much. Not only did it help me fall asleep soundly, but also it delighted me. After the required 21 days of carrying it out, I continued doing it almost every night.

It was my intention to continue my path as a Reiki healer and I was determined to go as far as I could. Therefore, to continue to learn the Reiki Level Two course had always been on my mind.

Quality control and a number of practices are a must in our teaching system. We, Reiki students were taught never to rush, but to take things steadily and naturally. In order to learn the level two course we needed a minimum practice of ten treatments on other people within at least three months.

Therefore, from the middle of December onwards, in addition to devoting most of my free time to writing, I also performed Reiki treatments on my friends, and even on our hotel guests. In total I performed 11 treatments.

I remember that three of them fell into a deep sleep after only five or ten minutes, which I found rather odd and almost unbelievable. Later on I discussed this with my teacher Begonia. She said that it was in fact a good sign, indicating that they had entered into a deeply relaxed state. Others didn't fall asleep but all of them reported that they could feel a kind of energy flowing in them, which felt warm and comforting.

Each time I finished a treatment, I felt a sense of wholeness and fulfillment, which strengthened my belief that to be a healer is defi-

The Twin Flame Lover of China and Denmark

nitely one of my soul's missions.

Traditionally, the focus of Reiki Level One is hands-on therapy at a purely physical level, both for self-treatment and for treating others. However, it is said that as we continue to practice, Reiki energy will continue to heal us and bring about changes in our life.

I remember Begonia had mischievously said to me, "Indigo, be prepared, changes will definitely come to you..."

Indeed, I remember that I gradually began to feel young and gentle. For the previous two years I had hardly ever let my hair down, because I didn't want to be so feminine. However, strangely and unexpectedly, I gradually wanted to dress and act in a more feminine way. I also felt more grounded and balanced. Consequently, my palms became even warmer than before and their sensitivity to energy automatically increased.

Deep down I felt happy about these positive changes.

About three months later, on March 19th and 20th, 2016, I and my Reiki friend Angelika went to Begonia's apartment to take our Reiki Level Two course.

Before the teaching started, Begonia said to me, "Indigo, I am delighted! Your face has changed, you look different now; much better, in fact. The first time I saw you there was a huge cloud of worry and sadness over your head..."

I truly felt happy to hear that and I felt grateful for her cheerful words. Meanwhile, I couldn't help thinking, "Dear Begonia, a few days before I met you I had talked with my beloved Oskar on the phone. If you knew the whole story, you would fully understand why the heavy cloud of worries and sadness was there. I think I actually acted quite bravely by not having asked God to quietly take my life away, like I did a few years ago. I have become a rather resilient and strong spirit, I think."

Reiki Level Two teaching and training was much more intense and deeper than Level One. Deep down Angelika and I knew we were getting into the core center of the matter and that we needed to prepare for the small and big changes that would definitely happen in our lives, as we continued to practice.

We were asked to perform a minimum of 30 treatments on other people during a minimum period of six months, if we wanted to pursue the Reiki Level Three course in the future. I definitely wanted to do that.

Again, the instructions for practicing were never to rush, but to develop ourselves based on our inner urge and our heart's rhythm.

It is also said that Reiki Level Two works not just on the physical level but the mental, emotional and spiritual areas as well. In other words, as we continued healing ourselves and others, we would definitely experience the purification of our physical, emotional, mental and spiritual bodies.

I remember that as my practicing continued, a number of profound changes definitely happened to me.

Before this, whenever I felt anger, hatred or any other negative emotions, I always suppressed them as quickly as possible, considering them "bad emotions." However, after taking the Level Two course, I gradually found that I could not bear holding any negative emotions within me at all, not even for few seconds.

My emotions had become quite childlike. When I was happy, I laughed; when I was angry, I showed my anger; when I felt sad or overwhelmed with emotions I couldn't clearly express, I allowed myself to cry.

In the eyes of most adults such behavior would be considered naïve, or even silly. However, I would like to think that it is important to be true to our emotions and, what is even more vital, to find healthy and non-harmful ways to express them properly. By doing so we can then live fully in the NOW and not get trapped in the cage of the past.

Another significant and profound change happened to my old thinking pattern. More specifically, it was reflected in my altered thoughts and new understanding about Oskar's past words and deeds.

For a long time I had felt rather angry and disappointed by his objection to my au pair plan. I had judged him to be lacking in courage and I had been putting the blame on him. Moreover, I often thought to myself that merely from his attitude it was clear enough that he probably just did not love me anymore.

The first time when my friend Wendy read about that chapter she wrote to me, "Oskar said to you that it was too risky. Perhaps he was saying it was too risky for you (not for him)! He was perhaps worrying about your situation, rather than his own!"

Back then, I simply considered Wendy was being kind to think in that way and I continued my old thinking pattern, living in the dense low energy of hurt and angry feelings.

As my heart chakra continued to open, I was gradually guided to think in a more understanding and compassionate way. Back then, before going to Denmark I had always imagined that to be an au pair was quite easy and enjoyable; only after the experience of being an au pair did I come to fully understand what it meant.

Clearly, Oskar knew what an au pair was supposed to do and it is likely that he had probably witnessed or heard some unpleasant stories about au pairs. He knew the "free spirit" aspect of my character and he understood my heart better than anyone else. To a large extent he knew I definitely would not enjoy my life as an au pair. And indeed, I did feel heavy and unhappy about my au pair work at the beginning, didn't I?

If, back then, I was still the one he deeply loved and cared about, he certainly would not have wished me to encounter any possible unhappiness in that situation. It could be that he rejected the idea out of consideration for me.

When we truly love someone, do we want them to sacrifice their own happiness, when we are fully aware that their sole purpose is to stay together with us?

And why did he run away from me?

I used to think, "Because he doesn't love me any more, because I am not good enough for him, so he wanted to find a better partner; because I have caused him too much pain and sorrow, he doesn't trust me any more. Some people say that the Twin Flame runners run because they have their own fears and problems, but it doesn't make any sense to me; I don't understand it!"

Again, those dense thoughts left me feeling deeply hurt and frustrated. However, as a deeper layer of healing and awakening happened, my mind began to think differently.

"Suppose he was really running away from himself, as people are known to do? When facing such an intense rare love, he could have been deeply shocked and began to think that everything that had happened was merely a drama, just like I used to think. He must have suffered as much as I did. I wasn't the only one in pain.

"Back then, neither of us had any well-thought-out career plan, especially me. It was easy to conclude that to build a solid future and live together was an impossibility. Could it be that he decided not to continue our relationship out of consideration for my future?"

No matter what the truth about Oskar might be, my heart has chosen to perceive him in this new way. In tears and love I let the anger and blame go, replacing it with compassion and forgiveness.

The old version of our story was, "Once upon a time, my beloved Oskar loved me deeply, more dearly than ever. But then he suddenly ran away because he did not love me any more. I was left to be feeling deeply hurt and abandoned. I didn't know how to continue living my life any more."

Now, the new version has become, "The fact that Oskar didn't return my love the way I wished doesn't necessarily mean he did not love me. Perhaps, the way I wanted was not the way that had been divinely planned for us. I need to release all my hidden expectations and secret plans which were made based on what I had thought was best for us and what I wished could happen. When I let go of my need to control, and detach myself from any possible outcomes, I become the wise self who is able to join the greater flow guided by

The Twin Flame Lover of China and Denmark

The Divine. My life will then eventually blossom in light and beauty."

Across time and space, I see myself working and teaching as a wonderful, shining Reiki Master Teacher...

Chapter 34

Becoming a Dancer

As the writing and healing was going on, I was also thinking: "How can I fulfill myself as a dancer? How can I bring joy and inspiration to people through my dancing?"

After thinking for some time I conceived of the idea of dancing in our hotel bar for our guests as my unique way to share love and light.

My first dance performance was scheduled around the middle of March, with the special intention of greeting and thanking Philip's parents, Torben and Malene. By that time, they had arrived in Beijing from Denmark to visit Philip and had checked into our hotel. Without Torben's kindness in introducing me to Philip, I might never have become a real healer. Thus, I found sufficient reasons and the courage to dance in public for the first time.

During my two work days I invited around 12 guests, with whom I felt a good connection. I did not tell them that I would be the dancer, though. I simply said to them, "Excuse me, M'am/Sir, tomorrow night there will be a special healing dance performance held in our hotel bar from 6 p.m. to 7 p.m. It is the first time we have organized this event. We, and the dancer herself feel quite excited about it. It is our trial performance. Audience reactions will help us to subsequently improve the event. If you are interested, you are more than welcome to join us…"

Yes, nearly all the guests whom I invited firmly said yes with a sense of delight and curiosity. This made me feel excited, but also a little nervous.

On the evening in question there were around 14 guests sitting in our hotel bar, including Torben and Malene. This was just the right number for the relatively small bar. My co-workers were there to help and support me, too, for which I felt genuinely grateful.

When all were ready, I gave the guests my personal introduction. "Good evening, ladies and gentlemen, welcome to our special healing dance performance tonight. We feel honored and happy to have you all here. I am Indigo, whom you met in the reception area. But also, I will be the dancer for you tonight…"

Hearing this, there was a kind of "Wow" response from my audience, which felt welcoming and encouraging. I realized it was a good surprise, instead of a horrible one. I felt relieved and relaxed.

Then, quite mischievously, I said to them, "It will make me feel very happy if you say you have thoroughly enjoyed my dance at the end. However, if you say you don't really like it at all, it will feel very fine to me. Because after all, after this performance, you will check out and we will perhaps never see each other again…"

"Ha ha ha…"

Hearing this laughter, I felt more relaxed. With confidence and love, I began my dance.

Initially I felt nervous, but quite soon I found my way to become a concentrated being who knew her mission was to channel higher love and light through her movements, and to share the higher energy contained in all she does, like any soul dancers do. I felt well and divinely inspired.

During the break between two pieces of music I thanked the audience with a gesture and they in turn offered their passionate applause. I understood it was an exchange of our appreciation of each other.

An undeniable deep sense of fulfillment and joy overwhelmed me while I was dancing. I knew deep down that it was my mission and was something I had wanted to do for a long time.

The Twin Flame Lover of China and Denmark

After the performance, people told me they truly enjoyed it and thanked me for offering them a special, different experience. I felt happy to hear that, but felt even happier to hear a lovely lady say to me: "You, Indigo! You are the star!"

It delighted my soul.

I didn't want to hold this performance regularly, merely as a way to entertain people, but rather to demonstrate the power and beauty of dance at the right time, whenever my heart prompted it.

Therefore, it was about two months later, some time during May, when I strongly felt an urge dance again for our guests. I and my co-workers held the performance for the second time and I was guided to carry it out in a better way.

After getting the approval of my manager Oliver, I wrote an invitation letter as follows:

Indigo's Healing Dance Performance Invitation

Indigo, our reception manager, whose real name is Defang Wan, went to Denmark in 2013 and stayed there for 11 months. During her time there, the combination of the beautiful Danish Fonix music and the unique emotions she experienced influenced her and awakened her innate dancing ability.

Without any prior dance training or learning experiences, a special new dance with the characteristics of Tai Chi, yoga and Latin, and featuring hand movements drawing spirals, was channeled through her.

She has been practicing this dance and has been experiencing its wonderful healing and transforming energy for three years. She would like to share this joy with you and she delights in inspiring and empowering you through this delicate and thoughtful dance.

Please feel welcome to join us for this special performance tonight from 6-7 p.m. at the hotel bar. We ask for nothing from you, but only your lovely open heart!

Best regards,
Hotel Management

The Twin Flame Lover of China and Denmark

Also, this time, when I was inviting guests at my reception, I honestly told them I would be the dancer. As expected, I heard many invisible "Wows" and happy, "Looking forward to it."

Beyond my expectation, there were about 24 guests who came that night, when in fact I remember that I had only invited about 18. But anyway, the more the better, I thought.

Before the performance really started, my co-workers and I gave the printed leaflet to our guests so they could read it, knowing that it would add more quality and a sense of dedication to what we were doing.

The music was more or less the same, the movements still felt familiar and connected, the atmosphere felt even higher and more passionate. We saw the improvements we had made and the areas we could do even better next time.

"Thank you, Indigo, for your lovely and special dance performance. Our family really enjoyed it very much. We believe you have a talent for dance, especially since it was you who created the dance. Can you sign your name both in Mandarin and English on your leaflet here? We'd like to keep it as a special memory of our trip to China..."

"Sure, of course! And thank you! Thank you for coming from Australia to Beijing to watch my dance!"

"Ha ha ha..."

With love and laughter I signed my name both in Mandarin and English on the leaflet, meanwhile, thinking, "I will continue holding my dance performances in the long run; and perhaps I will start learning a new type of dance that resonates with my heart and soul; life is like a beautiful dance and I need to learn how to do it with my unique charm and grace."

My spirit smiled in her understanding and knowing.

Chapter 35

What Will Happen Next?

Like you, dear readers, I, too, look forward very much to knowing the answers to this question. In fact, in addition to this question, I have many others in my heart as well.

Will this book find Oskar some day, somehow?

Are we the true Twin Flames, like I believe us to be?

Will I start writing my next book and what will it be about?

How will my path unfold as a healer and as a dancer?

What are my heart's true desires and soul's longings and how will I fully manifest them?

In what way can I serve the Great Spirit at a deeper level, resonating with a higher vibration?

These are the questions I care about and I do not yet know the answers. But as I continue my journey of evolution, as you do, I will always remember the divine words from the Spirit:

"Be true to your heart, listen to it and carry out its wise suggestions; have the courage to be different, to take risks so that you become the person who makes a significant difference to our world; be dedicated and have the courage and faith to trust that no matter what happens to you, it is for your highest good; finally, be diligent and back up your words and dreams with actual actions."

I know that, if we continuously live with this level of consciousness, the Great Happiness will eventually find its way to us.

See you in my next book!

STAGE SEVEN

Reunion of the Soul
(July 2016-Present Day)

By this stage, both twins have fully understood the very sacred nature of this divine relationship. Fear is replaced by trust, ego is banished by the light, the accumulated karma is resolved, all involved forces and powers begin to flow to work for the final reunion of the twins... After a long period of separation, they come together and fully embrace each other in their soul's home of love and joy. This is the lovely shining Rainbow Time of their reunion; the ultimate yin and the ultimate yang integrate their evolved energy into The Great Creator's energy, assisting the twins to fulfill their mission in divine love and Light...

The final chapter is yet to be written...

www.ingramcontent.com/pod-product-compliance
Lightning Source LLC
Chambersburg PA
CBHW030921090426
42737CB00007B/275